CHAOS IN THE SAND

A History of the XIII Corps at Alamein
The Southern Sector
October and November 1942

Barrie S. Barnes

Helion & Company

Helion & Company Limited
Unit 8 Amherst Business Centre
Budbrooke Road
Warwick
CV34 5WE
England
Tel. 01926 499 619
Email: info@helion.co.uk
Website: www.helion.co.uk
Twitter: @helionbooks
Visit our blog http://blog.helion.co.uk/

Published by Helion & Company 2019
Designed and typeset by Mary Woolley (www.battlefield-design.co.uk)
Cover designed by Paul Hewitt, Battlefield Design (www.battlefield-design.co.uk)

ISBN 978-1-912866-15-1

British Library Cataloguing-in-Publication Data.
A catalogue record for this book is available from the British Library.

For details of other military history titles published by Helion & Company Limited contact the above address, or visit our website: http://www.helion.co.uk.

We always welcome receiving book proposals from prospective authors.

Contents

List of Photographs

List of Maps

Chaos in the Sand

B.S. Barnes

There are flowers now they say at Alamein
yes flowers in the mine-fields now.
So those that come to view this vacant scene
where death remains and agony has been, will find the lilies grow
flowers and nothing that we know.
But this is not the place that we recall
the crowded desert crossed with foaming tracks
the one blotched building lacking half a wall.
The grey faced men sand powdered over all
the tanks, the guns the trucks, the black dark smoking wrecks.
So be it: none but us has known this land
El Alamein will still be ours
and those ten days of chaos in the sand.
Others will come who cannot understand
will halt beside the rusty minefield wires and find there only flowers.
So they rang bells for us at Alamein, bells which we could not hear.

Major William John Fletcher Jarmain
193rd Battery, 61st Anti-tank Regiment, Royal Artillery.
Killed in Action 26th June 1944, aged 33 years.
Buried in *Ranville* War Cemetery, France

This book is dedicated to the men XIII Corps, 8th Army, who fought at El Alamein.
Their service and sacrifice helped turn the tide of the war against Fascism.

Acknowledgements

I should like to thank the following people who have helped me over the years as I worked on this manuscript: All of the valued contacts built up over the years, who shared with me their valuable collections of photographs, manuscripts, books and recorded interviews. The numerous veterans interviewed over many years and all those who shared letters, documents, manuscripts and photographs relating to their war service. Judy, Mike, Peter and Sheila of the Carnegie Heritage Centre, Hull, for sharing their knowledge, sources and books with me. Brian Cook of the Carnegie Heritage Centre Hull for all his diligent research and help with sources and books. Helion & Company proprietor Duncan Rogers for putting me in touch with a contact in Greece. Yanis Prekatsounakis for his help with the history of the 1st Greek Brigade. Stefanos Moraitis for providing access to the archive of Captain S Tzanetis, 1st Greek Brigade archive.

Barrie S. Barnes

Glossary

AFV	armoured fighting vehicle
Alam	Arab term for a cairn/rock
Ammo	Ammunition
AP	Armour Piercing shells
Besa	Tank mounted machine-gun
Bomb happy	Shell-shocked
Bren	British light machine-gun
Bersagliere	Italian Infantry, recognisable by black plumes on their headgear
Bofors Gun	Quick-firing anti-aircraft gun
Box	British defensive position
Breda	Italian M30 light machine-gun
Bren Carrier	Small British armoured tracked vehicle
Brewing up	the act of making tea or a tank that is blazing fiercely with the crew still inside.
Bully	Corned beef ration tin
CLY	County of London Yeomanry
Coy	Company
CSM	Company Sergeant Major
DAK	Afrika Korps
Deir	Arab term for landscape depression
Devil's Garden	German minefield zones
DSO	Distinguished Service Order
Dud	Unexploded shell that failed to detonate on impact
Enfilade	Flanking fire.
FDL	Forward defensive line/location.
Hardtack	Flour, water and salt biscuit
HE	High explosive
Honey	M3 Stuart Light Tank
Hull down	Tank in a defensive posture that has been dug into the ground to present the smallest target possible whilst engaging the enemy
HQ	Headquarters.
I/C	In command, i.e. 2 I/C.
Iti	(pronounced eyetie) Italian soldier.

Jebel	Arab term for a hill.
Gerry/Fritz	German soldier.
Khamseen	Sandstorm
MC	Military Cross
Meat waggon	Ambulance.
MID	Mentioned in Despatches
MG	Machine-gun.
MM	Military Medal
MO	Medical officer
M &V	Maconochies brand tinned meat and vegetable stew
Morning Hate	Period of time when both sides would fire artillery/mortar shells at their opponents; those interviewed stated they could set their watches by this activity
NCO	Non-commissioned officer
Nebelwerfer	Multi-barrelled rocket launcher known to British troops as the 'Moaning Minnie' because of the doleful sound its projectiles made when launched.
O/C	Officer commanding.
OP	Observation post.
Portee	Truck with a gun mounted on its bed, though not permanently attached as a means of unloading quickly.
Provost	Regimental police.
Pt	Hill on map denoted metres, i.e., point 64.
RASC	Royal Army Service Corps.
Red Devils	Small Italian hand grenades
RSM	Regimental Sergeant Major.
RTR	Royal Tank Regiment.
Sangar	Make-shift dug in defensive emplacement in a rocky location with rocks and sandbags built up around it for extra protection.
Scorpion Tank	AFV fitted with a rotating drum at the front with heavy chains attached. Whilst spinning it would explode mines and booby traps as it moved forward and make a path through minefields and barbed wire for others to follow.
Sapper	Private in the Royal Engineers.
S Mine	German anti-personnel mine, it would not explode when stepped on but once released it would spring up to waist height then explode throwing out hundreds of shrapnel balls in all directions.
Spandau	German light machine-gun.
Stuka	Junker 87 dive bomber.

Sticky bomb	ST Grenade-anti-tank 74 Mk. Designed by Stuart Macrae in 1940, it consisted of a nitro-glycerine explosive charge covered with a sticky substance and enclosed within a glass sphere. On striking a tank, its delayed fuse detonated. Approximately 2. 5 million were manufactured.
Tracer	Bullet with pyrotechnic charge inserted into the base which could be seen in daylight and especially at night. Every fifth round was a tracer. This configuration allowed the shooter to discern where fire was landing.
Stonk	Heavy artillery barrage.
Tommy	British soldier.
Tommy cooker	Small British field cooker or German sobriquet for British tanks that burned fiercely with the crews still inside.
Very light	Signal flare
Wadi/Nullah	Arab term for a dried up river bed
WT	Wireless traffic/truck
18 Set	Portable wireless set
88	8.8cm German anti-aircraft and anti-tank gun. Originally designed for an anti-aircraft role until employed with devastating effect during the French campaign of 1940. No allied tank could withstand this most feared of weapons.

Introduction

In the early 1980s I began interviewing veterans of the Second World War, the bulk of these interviews have appeared in three of my books: Operation Scipio, The Sign of the Double T and the 50th at Bay. I was thinking I had used up my archive of interviews and was wondering what I could do next, as I rummaged through the files in my study I came across a file marked 'The 50th Division at El Alamein' and to my great joy I found it was more interviews I had done with men of the 50th Northumbrian Division and had forgotten about. 'The 50th at Bay' covers the exploits of the 50th Northumbrian Division from 1939 to September 1942 [the years of defeat] and 'The Sign of the Double T' covers the period from 1943 to 1944 [the years of victory] and their disbandment. I did not realise there was a gap in between each book: the Alamein battle. I then set about writing a history of the 50th Northumbrian Division covering the period July to November 1942, as I wrote and studied what had happened at Alamein it became obvious that the 50th were in a part of the southern line held by the XIII Corps of the Eight Army that was mentioned in certain publications but was neglected in its detail as the main focus of events and the major actions were fought in the north by XXX Corps: the Australians, New Zealanders, South Africans, 51st Highlanders and the 1st and 10th Armoured Divisions.

My work now began to expand as I looked at the other units in XIII Corps that held the line in the south from Ruweisat Ridge, the boundary between the two corps, to the 700 feet high Mount Himeimat on the extreme left flank. The other regiments soon came into focus as I looked at how all the units of XIII Corps interacted with each other and the purpose for which they were used by Montgomery. Those other units were 7th Armoured Division, 44th Home Counties Division, the 1st Greek Brigade and the 2nd Free French Brigade. The study progressed in an organic fashion and soon became a study of the whole of XIII Corps at Alamein, the fighting in this sector was intended to keep the 21st Panzer Division and the Italian Ariete Armoured Division in the south to prevent them moving north to block the main attack by XXX Corps.

Here is their story as told by the men at the sharp end. The battles of XIII Corps may not have been on the scale of the fighting in the northern coastal sector, but they were fierce bloody encounters nonetheless and the units they faced were manned by formidable and experienced infantry and paratroopers, backed up by anti-tank regiments, massed artillery and armoured Divisions. The heights of Mount Himeimat on the left flank was occupied by the hardened troops of the Italian Folgore Parachute

Division and any movement or attack by the British brought down a ferocious response from the German and Italian artillery massed in the rear areas. The whole of XIII Corps line was under direct and constant observation from Himeimat.

The men I interviewed so long ago have now passed away and I have grown old, when I read what they had said to me I can again hear their friendly voices and see their faces, so pleased that someone was taking an interest in their memories and their views. We laughed, drank tea and chatted for hours, at times the mood would change as they told me what they did as young men and many broke down in floods of tears. Some things they told me I was asked never to tell a living soul about, and I have honoured that request, these things do not appear in any book and will die with me when my time comes. Most of them never told the details they gave me to their families and on numerous occasions families have contacted me when one of my books has been published to say how astonished they were to find out what their relatives did. It was my privilege to have met so many of them and I hope that this study will stand testament to their younger lives and to their comrades who never came home.

Barrie S. Barnes
1st June 2019

1

Miteiriya Ridge July–August 1942

From 1940 to 1942 the desert war was a story of widely fluctuating fortunes with wide sweeping advances followed by retreats and reverses. The summer of 1942 saw for the Axis Forces a spectacular victory in the protracted battles of the Gazala Line, followed by the seizure of Tobruk with its great dumps of British materials. The British retreat, or 'Gazala Gallop', became a mad dash for the frontier with Panzer Army Afrika in hot pursuit. The stand at Mersa Matruh was overcome on 29th June and Rommel's victorious forces surged forward to the Alamein Line that took its name from an insignificant railway halt in the desert. Here in July and August 1942 the Axis advance was fought to a bloody standstill in what is referred to as the First Battle of Alamein.

Churchill, shaken after the humiliation of the loss of the Gazala Line and Tobruk, was determined to have a victory on the battle-field. This was now urgently needed to boost Britain's standing with her two major allies, America and Russia. In early August Churchill visited British Middle East Head-quarters in Cairo and decided it was time for a purge. On 15th August General Alexander replaced Auckinleck as Commander in Chief Middle East and General Bernard Montgomery was appointed to command the Eighth Army. At this time Churchill was nearing desperation as he knew full well that any protracted stalemate in the desert would affect his standing as a statesman both at home and abroad. The reverses of the past months had to stop, and Churchill thought Montgomery the man to do it with his reputation for ruthless efficiency. Churchill pinned his hopes on this arrogant, less than lovable leader of men in the hope that his killer instinct would bring about a decisive victory in 1942.

To the east of Mersa Matruh the Libyan plateau is dissected by numerous deep and steep sided Wadis, country over which Rommel's forces would have to travel as the terrain begins to narrow until at Alamein it is only 40 miles wide. This natural barrier has its right flank on the sea in the north with the left flank resting on the impassable sand seas of the Quattara Depression in the south. The only route that would now give access to Rommel's objective, Alexandria, was through this broken stony desert whose width had been reinforced with strong fortifications and wide

Eighth Army troops at Alamein await the arrival of the Afrika Korps. (Author's collection)

ranging minefields. The prepared and fortified British line at Alamein was a series of mutually supporting boxes, as at Gazala, which pivoted around the principal box bearing that name. Into these defences streamed the ragged remnants of Eighth Army passing through positions held by fresh and untried troops. The divisions that had been broken at Gazala and Mersa Matruh re-grouped and caught their breath as they once again stood at bay.

The numerical strengths of each side at this time were roughly equal but the morale of Panzer Army Afrika was much higher than Eighth Army for the Axis Forces could see before them a successful end to a hard campaign. Montgomery stationed XIII Corps in the important south west sector. The 22nd Armoured Division was stationed between the 2nd New Zealand Division and Alam Halfa Ridge. The 7th Motor Brigade was to patrol from the New Zealand position as far as Mount Himeimat in the extreme south and the light tanks and armoured cars of the 4th Light Armoured Brigade would patrol around Himeimat itself. The Desert Air Force was continually in action as it pounded the Axis Forces wherever they could find them.

An aircraft of the Desert Air Force flies low over a British patrol on its way to the enemy. (Author's collection)

Undaunted the Italian and German forces followed their leader into battle hoping for a decisive victory over a beaten enemy, Lt Pietro Ostellino of the Italian army wrote home to his wife:

> Things are getting better and better. As you will have heard from the radio and newspapers, the English and their allies are taking such a beating that they will find it difficult to raise their heads again, they deserve it. Our soldiers are simply marvellous, and we cannot fail to be victorious now.[1]

On 1st July 1942 at first light, after an all night drive, Rommel launched his weary forces against the British positions in an attempt to puncture the new British Line. His need to defeat the British was so desperate and rushed that he neglected any reconnaissance of the area, a mistake that would cost him and his forces dearly. His thrust was made astride the Miteiriya Ridge and through the gap south of the Alamein

1 M. Hastings. *All Hell let Loose.* (London: Harper-Collins 2011), p.176.

defensive box, intending that one wing of his army should swing north to envelope this position while the other wing swung south to take XIII Corps in the rear. This poorly thought out plan was badly executed, and the attack went completely awry. The left wing lost direction and instead of passing through the gap ran headlong into the Alamein Box, the Australians there poured a withering fire into the German ranks throwing them into a state of confusion and pinning them down with artillery and machine-gun fire. The German 90th Light Division was thrown into disorder and panicked and as they were about to flee the battle-field senior officers stepped in and restored order.

Tired and unshaven Panzer Grenadiers rest after coming out of action. (Courtesy of H Wernamann)

The right wing, which included 55 tanks of the 21st and 15th Panzer Divisions, ran into what they thought was an undefended box at Deir el Shein. This position was held by the 18th Indian Infantry Brigade, the 97th, 121st and 124th Field Regiments of the Royal Artillery, nine old Matilda infantry support tanks and an anti-tank company of the Buffs. Most of these were untried troops and control of the battle was lost at the start, two infantry battalions and some guns were overrun in the first shock of the German assault. General Nehring offered to accept the surrender of the remainder of the British garrison and sent a captured British officer in a Bren Carrier under a white flag to offer terms. What was left of the garrison refused the offer and stood fast, in the fiery heat of the day a bloody battle was fought out in the sand and rock of the desert, many German tanks were knocked out as they attacked, others moved into the British box but were hit by artillery fire as gunners fired over open sights. By nightfall the Germans had lost 18 tanks and were thoroughly shaken by this stubborn resistance. After dusk what was left of the British garrison withdrew, having received no support from any other formation. In those days such was the fate of an isolated and unsupported brigade group, echoes of the fate of 150 Brigade at Gazala.

British gunners firing over open sights into the advancing panzers. (Author's collection)

The box at Deir el Shein had been lost but the German spearhead had been blunted. The actions at the Alamein and Deir el Shein boxes marked the turning of the tide. The battle here continued with scarcely a days' intermission for over a month. Rommel was constantly seeking a weak spot where he could break through and Auckinleck counter attacked his every move. In the stifling heat of the desert fighting of the most savage kind took place and losses on both sides were great.

Many Italian units broke and fled or were taken prisoner. Rifleman Thomas Arthur Murray of the Rifle Brigade remembers being shocked at the youth of some of the men who gave themselves up:

> We took numbers of Italian and German soldiers, obviously shell-shocked, a condition we called 'bomb happy', giving themselves up, no doubt through the

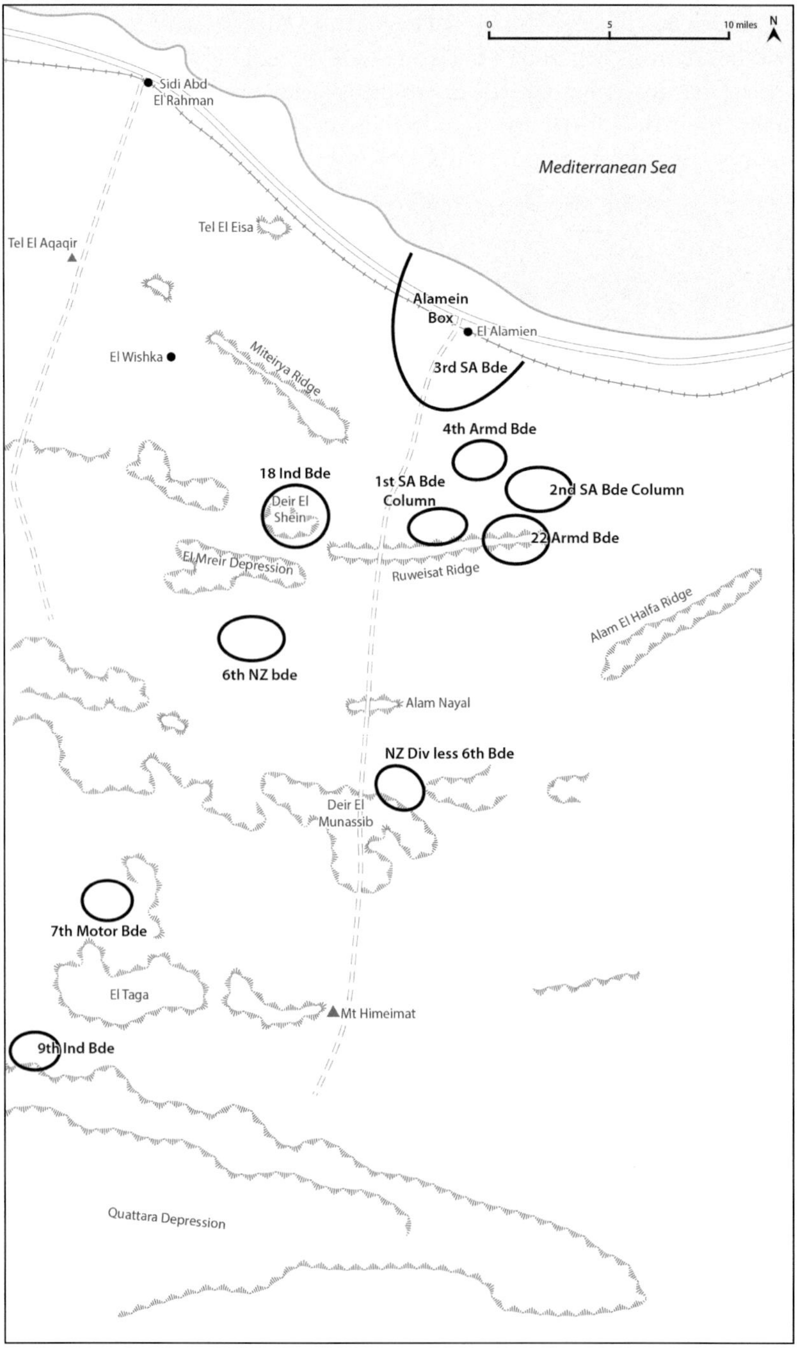

Alamein July 1942.

> tremendous barrage they had experienced. It was a shock to realise how young these soldiers were and for me it was an indication of how bad things were for the Axis armies that they could send such youngsters into battle.[2]

Not all Italian troops gave up the struggle so easily and many individual units stood their ground in the most trying circumstances. Major Renzo Rastrelli was with the Sabratha Division:

> The enemy was close at hand and their patrols and armoured cars were all over the road. Without hesitation the battery commander, Captain Comi, opened fire at minimum elevation, handling his massive 149s as if they were machine-guns. The space before the levelled guns was swept clear in no time. The ground was ploughed up in front of the guns for a distance of close on 200 yards, the guns became red hot and many of the handlers were burnt. The area in front of Comi was deserted except for blazing vehicles and dead Australians.[3]

Both sides were now being reinforced, the British more strongly than the Germans. The 9th Australian Division arrived from Syria and took over the coastal sector making a number of attacks, they captured Tel el Eisa and Miteiriya Ridge but could not hold them. More important were the savage battles to take Ruweisat Ridge, its rocky crests were torn apart by the vicious detonations of countless exploding shells giving the infantry no hiding place. The New Zealanders and the Indians attacked this hellish place twice but could not hold it. The ridge and its flanks were littered with the corpses of both sides as the battle flowed and ebbed, masses of flies crawled over the rotting bodies.

On 2nd July a mixed force consisting of the Queen's Bays, 9th Lancers and 4th Hussars [armour] under the command of Lord Knebworth of the Bays, repelled an attack by 30 enemy tanks. This composite force did the same again on 4th July and Lord Knebworth was killed.

Captain Vernon Northwood commanded A Company, 2/8th Battalion, 9th Australian Division:

> It was about one o clock in the morning and I saw a gun being pulled up on to a ridge. I thought it couldn't be one of ours as it was being brought up on the wrong side of the ridge about 40 yards away. I watched as two truck loads of men came up and I realised it was an 88mm gun. I turned my company to face them and said we must go in with the bayonet, quickly I got two platoons

2 Manuscript sent to author by T.A. Murray, 1993.

3 J. Thompson. *Desert Victory* (London: Ebury Press 2012), p. 235.

Rommel and his commanders plan the next move. (Courtesy of H Wernamann)

forward as men were getting in position to defend the gun. I couldn't wait for the third platoon and shouted 'into them', for a moment I was the only man on my feet and thought I was the only one to go, I got a fright. I was shouting like a madman. You know that if the enemy are in a position to run they will, they won't face you, especially if they are lying in the open and not in a trench. I heard this noise behind me, all my men shouting and screaming, it was frightening. I only got a few paces when I took a bullet through the top of my steel helmet just above the forehead and scraped the top of my scalp, then one through the top of my arm, I thought I would lose it. It was like being kicked by a horse, I have been kicked by a horse in the past. Then wham! One through my neck, a flesh wound. I was thrown down and dropped my rifle and bayonet, somebody shouted 'the skipper's hit', I said 'I'm alright' as I didn't want them to stop. They got to where the gun had been which had gone, and I could see my men taking prisoners. Had the gun got into position it would have covered the rear of the ridge. I found I was able to walk and the company orderly came with me as I was a bit groggy.[4]

4 Manuscript sent to author by V. Northwood 1989.

Stricken Panzers burning furiously before the Australian positions. (Courtesy of Wilfred Gilson)

This bitter and confused fighting in July, often referred to as First Alamein, was in fact the concluding part of the Battle of Gazala and if this is not a separate battle it is still of great significance despite glaring faults of many of Auckinleck's subordinate commanders. Although the British failed to throw the enemy back they did put a stop to his advance. By the end of July both sides were exhausted having fought each other to a standstill. The British were now superior in numbers but there were serious problems at command level. Military failures are by no means always due to the shortcomings of the generals, quite often it is the troops that are the problem, but in Eighth Army the troops were of a particularly high standard. Many had been severely tested in the ferocious Gazala battles of May and June, but the fighting spirit of Eighth Army remained un-impaired, with the exception of new arrivals they were an army of young veterans and were skilled craftsmen on the battle-field. For the most part they were tenacious and resilient, and their understanding of combat was exceptional.

The men of the 50th Division had played their part in all of this, losing more than their fair share of troops in the Gazala Line and during the retreat to Alamein, they lost 9,000 casualties in the months of May and June. Back in the Delta their commanders took stock of the situation and found the division was not in good shape. 40 percent of the field artillery pieces had been lost, the 72nd Field Regiment, along with 150 Brigade, had been lost in the desperate last stand at Gazala and all the supporting arms had taken heavy casualties. The infantry suffered worst, the two brigades that remained,

The Desert Air Force harried the enemy wherever they could be found. (Author's collection)

69 and 151, had an average battalion strength of 300 men. However morale remained high as the troops set about the task of re-organisation and rebuilding. On 11th July Major General John Sebastian [Crasher] Nichols, DSO, MC, took command of the division and reinforcements arrived for the badly depleted infantry. Both brigades entered a phase of intense training in the Ameriya area.

There was to be no rest period for the men of the 50th Division as on 15th July orders were received to begin reserve defences east of Ruweisat Ridge, the 21st Indian Brigade and a motorised infantry brigade came under divisional command to perform similar work in the same area. The troops worked hard and by the evening of the 18th July the major part of the new defences was complete. Sgt Max Hearst of the 5th Battalion East Yorkshire Regiment says of that time:

> In July we slaved like blacks under a blazing sun to complete these defensive positions, what a fucking job, but we knew it was important to get these works finished, we expected Gerry tanks to appear at any moment and that made us work harder. It wasn't long before we were moved to the front with the Indians alongside of us.[5]

5 Interview with author. Max Hearst, Hull 1992.

Sergeant Max Hearst as a young recruit, 5th Battalion East Yorkshire Regiment. (Courtesy of Max Hearst)

69 Brigade was then ordered to move forward and come under the command of 5th Indian Division on Ruweisat Ridge, they were to take up defensive positions on the ridge by first light on 19th July in case of any breakthrough by the enemy, part of their brigade group included the 2nd [machine-gun] Battalion the Cheshire Regiment and the 233rd Field Company, Royal Engineers. On 20th July new orders were received and the brigade was on the move again to come under the command of 7th Armoured Division. It was their task to attack the Taqa Plateau and Jebel Kalakh in the south of the sector held by 7th Armoured Division, a composite battalion from 201st Guards Brigade was to be placed under the command of 69 Brigade. If this attack was a success the 4th Light Armoured Brigade of the 7th Armoured Division, was to pass through the gap and work behind the enemy forcing him to withdraw. The divisional artillery would be in support for all phases of this attack. The commander of 69 Brigade, Brigadier Cooke-Collis, DSO, found no intelligence about the area over which they were about to attack, and little was known about the situation on Taqa Plateau and Jebel Kalakh. Reconnaissance was impossible in daylight hours as the whole area was under enemy observation and any movement brought down artillery fire. It was

clear that the troops available were in no condition to carry out a major operation of this kind, 69 Brigade was a composite force that had been scratched together and the Guards battalion was very much under strength and had been involved in heavy fighting already. It was decided that the Guards should attack and capture the east end of the Taqa Plateau as it was thought to be weakly held and would be within the powers of this rather under strength battalion. At 23:00 p.m. on 21st July the Guards reached their objective without any difficulty. At 01:30 a.m. on 22nd July the 6th Battalion Green Howards on the right and 5th Battalion East Yorkshire Regiment on the left began their advance at first light. No enemy was encountered as they reached the southern edge of the plateau but with the light of day came heavy machine-gun fire and mortar fire. Both battalions spent a most unhappy day on this plateau but could make no more headway and the casualties mounted as artillery fire and mortar fire fell upon their positions, some of the men were by now suffering from heat exhaustion.

25 Pounder gun crew in action. (Courtesy of Wilfred Gilson)

Company Sergeant Major Allan Potter, D Company, 2/28th Battalion, 9th Australian Division was in the thick of the action at Miteiriya Ridge and watched the progress of 69 Brigade:

> We dug in and didn't have a great deal of time. There wasn't much cover and when first light came so did the German infantry on half-tracks who dismounted and advanced on us. This time we had enough ammunition to repel two infantry attacks. The battalion had advanced and had taken the ridge, it was planned that a tank regiment would come up on each side of us and 69 Brigade, 50th Division, would cover our front, it looked easy. The enemy had destroyed most of our support coming through the minefield and we were

running out of ammunition. We had to rely on the tanks, these tanks started to advance to join us but were driven off by 88s. All we saw of them on the flanks was a lot of dust and them retreating, so we didn't get the tank support. We were sitting there like Aunt Sallys. The British 69 Brigade which was to come across our front ran into trouble straight away and by the time they had reached their objective they must have been all but annihilated. Then we saw help coming, tanks were approaching from our right front, they appeared to be our tanks. At this point Jimmy Allen got the idea he would take an anti-tank vehicle and guide them into our position, and he raced past my sangar, about 75 yards out a German shell landed on his vehicle and blew him clean out of it. He landed on his back and I raced across to him to see what I could do. He was split right up through the body and he asked me to shoot him, I said 'don't worry Jim' but what could I do. I went back to my sangar as I didn't have enough shell dressings to bind up such a large wound. The German tanks were getting closer and closer, firing all the time. The company commander asked, 'what's happening?' I told him Jim was badly hit and wanted me to shoot him. But by now the enemy tanks were getting really close.[6]

A British Jock Column moving over the rough desert terrain. (Author's collection)

6 J. Sadler, *El Alamein* (Stroud: Amberley Publishing. 2012), p. 166.

Throughout the day it was obvious that the enemy was reinforcing their units in the area and by 16:00 p.m. the expected counter-attack fell on both battalions supported by armoured cars. The infantry of 69 Brigade poured a withering fire of mortar shells onto the advancing Germans and the divisional artillery laid down a ferocious barrage that halted the attack. On the night of the 22nd July fighting patrols were sent out into no-man's land by both battalions, the information gathered showed more German units were moving into the area to renew the assault. During the 23rd July both battalions were subjected to heavy concentrations of artillery and mortar fire and the enemy counter-attacked twice, the brunt of these attacks was taken by 5th Battalion East Yorkshire Regiment causing many casualties. Pte Harry Forth of the 5th Battalion East Yorkshire Regiment watched events unfold:

Pte Harry Forth, 5th Battalion East Yorkshire Regiment and his wife Rene. (Courtesy of Harry Forth)

> Gerry was moving his tanks and vehicles about quite a bit, we could hear them and see the clouds of dust thrown up, to say the least this was a bit disconcerting. That night we went out on a fighting patrol led by Lt Sykes, as we advanced in the dark it was easy to imagine every shadow was a German lying in wait for us, as our eyes got used to the low light we could see shapes in the distance but we never got too close, all we had to do was to look out for enemy patrols and for concentrations of tanks and vehicles, which we did. After a scary night in

> no-man's land we returned to our own lines unmolested as light broke. Gerry attacked our positions more than once, shells exploded around us and in the distance we could see tanks and lorried infantry approaching. The response to this was a major stonk [barrage] on the advancing Germans, the effect was to break up the advance of the panzers and it left many burning tanks scattered about the desert. Although we were glad they had not reached our positions we could not help but feel sorry for the men under this terrible bombardment.[7]

After a cold night, Tommies in slit trench keep a watchful eye for the enemy. (Author's collection)

On the night of 23rd/24th July Lt Colonel Sammy Battiscombe led a composite DLI battalion on a night attack, the Germans let them pass and then cut off their line of retreat. The promised tank support failed to materialise, and the troops were captured along with their Commanding Officer.

The same night the badly mauled battalions of 69 Brigade withdrew from their positions without any interference from the enemy and re-joined the 50th Division. The men were suffering from severe strain after the ferocious heat of the plateau, the lack of food and water and the trials caused by areas of soft sand that bogged down

7 Interview with author, H. Forth, Cottingham 1989.

Lt Colonel S. Battiscombe. 9th Battalion Durham Light Infantry. (Courtesy of Ralph Hymer)

heavily laden vehicles all of which had to be dug out by the men. The rifle companies had been reduced to a third of their original strength and before they could get any rest new recruits poured into the ranks to make good their losses. The following days were spent re-equipping the men and repairing vehicles and weapons. Once again orders were received to move off and on 25th July the division dug in in the Alam el Dakar sector.

On the night of the 26th July the 50th Division Stood To in preparation to move forward through the minefield gap, the 6th Battalion the Green Howards leading with the 5th Battalion East Yorkshire Regiment and the composite Durham Brigade following. They were to widen the minefield gap so that tanks could pass through and as they worked in the blazing sun the enemy plastered the gap with artillery fire causing more casualties.

British tanks arrived on 27th July but did not pass through the minefield gap, they stopped to the rear of 69 Brigade and throughout the day attracted the unwelcome attention of Stuka dive bomber formations and artillery fire. In the early evening enemy tanks attacked in force, passing through the gap made by the men of 69 Brigade, they outnumbered and outgunned the British tanks in the battle that ensued, and 69 Brigade was caught between the opposing forces. This operation was confused and poorly planned.

A German anti-tank gun team in a rare quiet moment. (Author's collection)

Lt Colonel G.W. Eden, 7th Battalion Green Howards, recalled:

> The difficulty of getting ones bearings in the desert at first light, when one has advanced in the dark over ground that one has not had the chance to look at previously, holding positions under fire all day without being able to make a reply, tanks unable to keep up because of enemy mines and merely drawing more fire and the spectacular effects of enemy dive bombing attacks. It is hard to describe the wonderful refreshment a cup of tea provides under such circumstances and, lastly, the steadiness of the men in our companies when ordered to withdraw was inspirational.[8]

After this action 69 Brigade re-joined the 50th Northumbrian Division at Alexandria.

As the fighting for Ruweisat Ridge died down Rommel was now forced to admit that he was facing an Eighth Army that was in the hands of a new commander who deployed his forces with considerable skill. It was not Rommel who was now calling the shots and instead he was made to dance to someone else's tune. The First Battle of Alamein was over, the Eighth Army had wrested the initiative from Rommel and had stopped his forces. The belief that Rommel was not invincible began to take root although there was still a long road to travel and much hard fighting to be done if he was to be defeated.

8 Manuscript by G.W. Eden 1992.

2

Alam Halfa 31st August–1st September 1942

In August 1942 Rommel had 10 divisions in the field compared to seven British divisions. The key to the Battle now being fought was two ridges, the most important one being Alam Halfa Ridge 10 miles east of the second which was Ruweisat Ridge. From the latter observation from its summit allowed its occupants to control the course of the fighting. Six Axis divisions struck at the British forces holding the southern end of the line, on the left of which was the 700 feet high Mount Himeimat, a mere pimple on the map but one of tactical importance. On 31st August Rommel launched his forces on a local offensive against positions prepared by Auckinleck at Alam Halfa.

A shot down Stuka dive bomber pictured at the moment of impact. (Author's collection)

2nd Lt Richard Tryon was with the 4th County of London Yeomanry, 7th Armoured Division, in late August as the attack went in:

> The Germans seem to love an evening scrap and at 18:00 p.m. there were German tanks emerging from the low ground ahead with their commanders well out of their turrets, they appeared to be forming up at 2,000 yards to attack, four rows deep with some big chaps with nasty looking guns at the front. There are 60 facing our squadron and a lot more to the right. Before we start firing we lose a tank, Heyday 1 is on fire and he is bailing out, he has a dead man in the tank and one or two wounded. The Germans are falling back now, they have failed to get through and they are leaving some 20 dead tanks behind them. They have had a nasty knock and we have lost many men.[1]

Sergeant Jake Wardrop was serving with the 5th Battalion Royal Tank Regiment, 7th Armoured Division, as the German armour came on:

> One night we beat off an attack by tanks, what a party! There were about 30 of them coming down the valley but we shook them. Lt Colonel Jim Hutton, C/O 5th RTR [nicknamed Fearless Jim] was talking on air 'here they come, hold your fire a bit longer, now let them have it, that's the stuff'. We certainly shook them up, we knocked out 15 tanks.[2]

Captain Oliver Woods, 4th County of London Yeomanry, watched the enemy tank formations advance:

> Just now a slight breeze began to blow up a minor sandstorm threatening to destroy visibility. Through it the light vehicles of the 7th Armoured Division, portees, carriers and light tanks, began to pass across our front as they skilfully drew on the enemy. Our own cruiser squadron, which had been sent out to join them, peeled off and wheeled back through the regimental tank line. Suddenly the dust dropped and the long line of telegraph poles which ran across our front and down to the south was visible in the clear light of a desert evening. Coming straight down it and heading towards us was a solid phalanx of German tanks stretching away as far as the eye could reach. At that distance they looked rather like black snails gliding across the sand. At one moment they stopped and those in the rear made off towards the east, but those in front, 80 to 100 strong, moved away from the wires and motored on until they were opposite our front

1 Manuscript sent to author by C. Mount 1992.
2 Letter to Author from C. Spandler Hull 1991.

Sergeant Jake Wardrop, 5th Battalion Royal Tank Regiment. (Courtesy of W Ridley)

British troops pose for a picture next to a knocked out panzer. (Author's collection)

> but just out of range, where they halted. The enemy tanks appeared to take on a corporate identity, as though they had noticed us for the first time and were wondering whether to go on or attack.[3]

Captain Woods watched the progress of the enemy formations with excited interest and as he looked on the panzers formed onto six lines and turning left headed for the positions held by 4th County of London Yeomanry. The artillery on a ridge to the rear of the British positions opened fire on the advancing enemy formation and shells exploded among the panzers. Undaunted the tanks advanced straight up the line of telegraph poles and came to a halt 800 yards from the British. It was at this point the British tank units received permission to open fire. Both sides now got an unpleasant surprise, the Germans did not realise the British held such well-prepared positions and that each gunner knew the exact range of each telegraph pole. In a matter of minutes many panzers were hit, turrets went flying into the air as black clouds of smoke rose into the sky. The surprise for the British was just as nasty, for the first time in the desert war the Mark VI Special was brought into action. A 75mm gun had been added to

British light tanks advancing. (Author's collection)

3 Manuscript sent to author by Oliver Woods 1994.

the normal Mark VI close support tank and these specials led the attack and could now penetrate the armour of a Grant Tank at 800 yards. The squadron on Captain Woods' right was concealed by a small knoll but the sound of battle could be heard clearly as the German force smashed into them, they had orders to fight to the last and as they stood their ground the Mark VI Specials took a heavy toll of the British tanks. Columns of black smoke rose into the sky from behind the knoll stretching away to the south like funeral pyres. The survivors could be observed dodging and scrambling up the ridge to safety.

Captain Oliver Woods:

> The battle was now at its hottest and great assistance was given to the tanks by the six pounder anti-tank guns of the Rifle Brigade. The Rifles were serving their guns interspersed in the tank line, loading and firing for all they were worth without benefit of armour in the middle of an armoured battle. A number of our tanks were manned by American crews who had come out to get combat experience. It was noticeable that the rear tanks were not moving up to take the place of the ones in front that had been knocked out. Then an astonishing thing happened as the sun moved very close to the horizon in its last light, the ground between the German tanks was covered with dismounted enemy crews, they were hitching tow ropes onto the disabled tanks. We let fly at them with machine-gun and high explosive and as the light faded the whole German force began moving backwards until it was out of range of our now empty guns, leaving behind them a squadron's worth of blackened smoking wrecks on the ground.[4]

Brigadier Roberts described the advance of the Axis armour:

> On they came, a most impressive array. I warn all units over the air not to fire until the enemy are within 1,000 yards, it can't be long now and in a few seconds the tanks of the CLY [County of London Yeomanry] open fire and the battle is on. Once one is in the middle of a battle time is difficult to judge, but it seems only a few minutes before nearly all the tanks of the Grant Squadron of the CLY are on fire. The new German 75mm is taking a heavy toll. The enemy have halted and they have had their own casualties, but the situation is serious; there is a hole in our defences. I hurriedly warn the [Scots] Greys that they must move at all speed and plug the gap. The enemy tanks are edging forward again and they have got close to the Rifle Brigade's anti-tank guns. When they open up they inflict heavy casualties on the enemy, but through sheer weight of

4 Manuscript sent to author by Oliver Woods 1994.

> numbers some guns are overrun. Artillery fire is called for and it comes down almost at once on top of the enemy tanks. This together with the casualties they have already received checks them.[5]

A German half-track tows an 88 out of action. (Author's collection)

Since taking over command of the Eighth Army Montgomery had done much to strengthen the British line and had made it quite clear to his subordinate commanders that there was to be no retreat. Ever since the fall of Tobruk Rommel had been putting the retreating British under pressure to prevent them from forming a stable front behind which they could organise the land and air reinforcements they were likely to receive. Auckinleck had striven to keep the Eighth Army in being for although it had suffered severe losses in men and materials it was only stunned and disorganised rather than demoralised. The Eighth Army was still capable of further efforts in the field and its initial framework was still intact, however this did not alter the fact that it was in a last ditch position. It was obvious that Rommel would waste no time in making his next move no matter how exhausted his troops might be. The task now before the Eighth Army and the Desert Air Force was clear: they must at all costs stop Rommel's troops from breaking through the British defences.

The halting of Rommel's troops in July 1942 was felt to be a great defensive victory, but soon the realisation set in that little had been achieved in the long term. After two

5 R. Kershaw, *Tank Men* (London: Hodder and Stoughton, 2008), p. 295.

years of fighting the British were back where they had started. Montgomery was now in command of the Eighth Army and he began to marshal his forces in no uncertain manner. He was determined to kick Rommel's forces out of Africa and instigated many changes in his command, he coordinated the movements of his ground troops and the Desert Air Force, and divisions were to fight as divisions with no fragmentation of effort. He decided never to attack until all contingencies had been broached, that he had a numerical superiority over his opponents and all his troops were trained and equipped to the highest standard. His orders were to be followed to the letter without complaint. The wind of change was blowing through the Eighth Army and everyone could feel it. In July and August both sides built up their forces.

Rommel knew that time was not on his side and his reconnaissance units reported the construction of vast minefields by the British and the building up of their defences, especially in front of Ruweisat Ridge and in the coastal sector. The short supply lines of the British meant that they were winning the race to build up supplies of men and materials and were growing stronger by the day. Rommel, with his extended supply lines, was now finding it difficult to get materials transported across the Mediterranean in order to build up an effective force. He was left with no alternative but to attack at once or face an even stronger enemy. A full moon was forecast for the 26th August.

A German heavy artillery piece in action. (Author's collection)

L/Cpl P B Ewings, 1/5th Queen's Regiment:

> In late August we moved into positions on Ruweisat Ridge in the southern part of the Alamein positions. We knew Rommel would try to push through towards the Nile at any time and we were supposed to hold him off. When the attack finally came at the end of the month however we were merely spectators, although we held firm in our positions in the face of heavy shelling and dive-bombing attacks. We had a perfect vantage point for the whole proceedings and what a show. Rommel's tanks were gradually driven back with great loss beyond the minefields and we felt a little safer.[6]

Rommel assembled his assault forces by night and camouflaged them through the day in order to gain the element of surprise and so mask the direction of the attack. Diversionary raids would be launched by the Italian units in the north, he thought his plan of breaking through the British Lines at Alam Halfa was sound and that it would then be possible to unleash the Afrika Korps to outflank and defeat the British

A British anti-tank gun being towed into position. (Author's collection)

6 Manuscript sent to author by P.B. Ewings 1991.

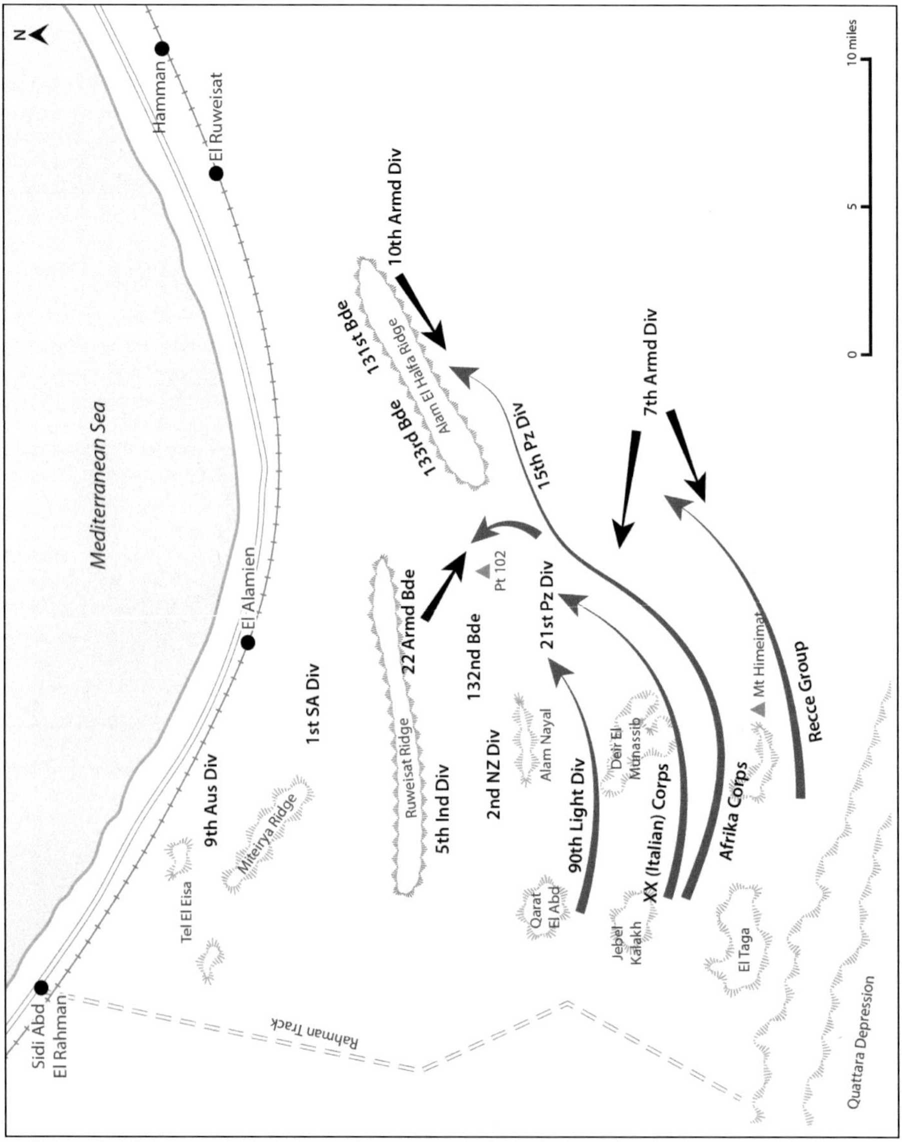

The Battle of Alam Halfa, 30th August to 1st September 1942.

in the old tried and trusted method. The plan was however obvious to his opponents who had taken steps to counter it, removing any element of surprise. Montgomery strengthened his forces on the all-important Alam Halfa Ridge and this feature would be the key to the battle. For Rommel this was his last chance to gain a quick and decisive victory that would enable him to break through to the Nile Valley.

Cpl Harold Wilmhurst was with the 5th Battalion Royal Sussex Regiment, 132 Brigade, 44th Home Counties Division, attached to the 2nd New Zealand Division:

> Our division was called forward to man positions on Alam Halfa Ridge, we had just arrived in Egypt from England. You could see for miles around and it was rocky, couldn't dig far down, the Royal Engineers had dug deep trenches for us. When the Germans attacked we stopped them, our first casualty was the OC of the pick-up truck who was blown up. The German planes came over and attacked us, we had three Bofors Guns protecting us and they put up a terrific barrage. Over 20 planes were shot down that day all around us. As the German aircrew came down on parachutes a Polish tank regiment near us shot them as they descended, killing them. We lay low in our slit trenches. Then C Company went forward with some tanks of the 23rd Armoured Brigade, they took over the ground in daytime and we took over at night while they re-fuelled. The Germans retreated and we followed up, as they retreated the RAF bombed them. We were attached to the West Kents who had taken a lot of casualties, we returned to our hill and on the way passed through the 4th Battalion Royal Sussex who had taken a pasting and they cheered us as we went back.[7]

Lt Ken Kettle, MC, was in command of the mortar platoon of the 1/6th Queens Regiment, 131 Brigade, 44th Home Counties Division. He struggled to get his mortar teams forward to their positions from which they could support the forward companies:

> Three battalions of the Queens moved onto Alam Halfa Ridge, some 15 miles behind the front. It was undoubtedly the key to the whole position and any right hook by Rommel must capture it to be successful. The battalions' dug-in, hard work in this rocky ground. There was an effective minefield surrounding the position and it was ordered that the ridge should be held to the last. The 44th Home Counties Division, the New Zealand Division and the 7th Armoured Division formed the southern part of XIII Corps of the army. The attack came in the south as expected and throughout the 31st August the 15th

7 Manuscript sent to author by J. Young Devon 1992.

and 21st Panzer Divisions, the 90th Light Division and the armoured Italian Corps advanced through our minefields [marked January, February, 'Nuts' and 'May' on the map], between Munassib and Himeimat. They were immediately engaged by our lighter forces. Here they were checked by our heavy armour, strongly attacked from the air and violently shelled by our artillery. During this battle 131 Brigade closed the minefield gaps and were subjected to dive-bombing attacks and the continuous shelling of their front. This vital battle has attracted little attention, but if it had been lost we might have lost Egypt.[8]

British anti-tank gun team in action. (Courtesy of Harry Forth)

At Alam Halfa 131 Brigade lost 700 casualties in the heavy fighting, whilst attached to the 2nd New Zealand Division.

For Montgomery it was to be his introduction to the North African Campaign and his first battle in command of the Eighth Army. On the night of 30th/31st August the tanks of the Afrika Korps passed through their own minefields only to blunder into unknown belts of British mines that held them up, the German engineers and infantry tried to deal with the thousands of mines and booby traps that littered a wide area and as they did this were met by a hail of shells from the British artillery. Relays of heavy bombers rained down death on the stationary tanks and vehicles of the Afrika Korps

8 *BBC World War II Peoples War Stories* <www.bbc.co.uk/history/ww2peopleswar/stories> (Accessed 19 September 2016).

as the 7th Armoured Division made a fighting withdrawal as planned. By dawn the German forces had not reached their objectives and the British could now plot the route of the attack and be fully prepared to receive the expected armoured thrust.

Lt Martin Highfield, 74th Field Regiment, Royal Artillery, recalls:

> We were called forward and on this occasion didn't support the 50th Division but supported the 22nd Armoured Brigade. We were in action the next day. The brigade had beaten off the German tanks overnight, a contributory factor was in the air and formations of our bombers strafed the advancing armour of the 15th Panzer Division. This was very heartening, and we realised that, for the first time in the war, the balance of air power was changing in our favour.[9]

The delays caused by the minefields and by formations of marauding British bombers caused Rommel to change his original plan, the British were alert and ready so Rommel changed tac and sent his attack formations left before they reached Alam Halfa Ridge earlier than had been previously planned, having reached their new objectives the panzers would then drive northwards behind Reweisat Ridge and on to the coast road. Before he could begin this plan his armour and vehicles would have to halt to re-supply, take on ammunition and re-fuel. Many Axis units were thrown into disarray as this attack faltered, the 15th and 21st Panzer Divisions had come up against two armoured brigades in defensive positions from which they raked the advancing Germans with tank and anti-tank gun fire causing tremendous damage.

Rifleman Thomas Arthur Murray was with the 1st Battalion Rifle Brigade:

> We heard the heavy sound of motors in the distance and soon after we saw German tanks coming at us. When they were 200 yards away they stopped and opened up on us, simultaneously the heavy guns to our rear opened up on them and very quickly about six of the tanks took hits and began to burn fiercely. All of our trucks were burning, and jeeps were being thrown into the air by the fire from these tanks. The heat from the closest burning tank was so fierce I could feel the skin being lifted from my face.[10]

Rifleman Douglas Waller, 1st Battalion Rifle Brigade:

> There were two of us in front and the other two were on our flanks and further behind us. They put us out there and said mark something 300 yards away, well we put an empty petrol tin there and they said that's your maximum range.

9 Letter to author from M. Highfield 1990.
10 Letter to author from T.A. Murray 1991.

Knocked out panzers and burning vehicles on the battlefield. (Author's collection)

> We were dug into these positions at Alam Halfa when we saw an armoured car come whizzing back to warn us tanks are coming. We sat there and waited and could eventually see them, about 70 of them. The first tank started moving when the commanders tank came up and very obligingly almost stopped on top of this petrol tin we'd put out. Nothing had happened yet, so we fired, and he was a goner because he was side on. Once we had fired the other tanks started firing at us. One came up and two of the crew bailed out of this one to get on the back of this other tank. We fired at it but the shells just bounced off the front, so we fired at the turret and the tracks, but it still kept going, as it started backing away its machine-guns opened up on us and the bullets went through the front shield of our gun and deflected off the curved shield behind. It also knocked the sights off our gun. Nobody was hit but if it hadn't been for that shield we'd have all been goners.[11]

The fierce fighting continued without pause and grew in intensity. Senior German officers died at the head of their men as they struggled to carry out Rommel's orders. Bismarck of the 21st Panzer Division fell and the commander of the Afrika Korps, Nehring, was wounded. Slowly the Germans and Italians beat their way forward losing

11 Manuscript sent to author by T. Brooks Cheltenham 1994.

men and tanks as they did so. The Germans now found out what it was like to attack well prepared defensive positions of anti-tank guns and armour. The British were now battle wise to German tactics and refused to be drawn out of their hull down positions, much to the annoyance of Rommel. As the light faded the attack was called off and the panzers withdrew to re-fuel and re-arm from their dwindling stocks.

Lt Harold Limer, 2 Troop, A Squadron, 44th Battalion Royal Tank Regiment, was awoken in the early hours to follow up as the German forces pulled back:

> When the enemy withdrawal began I was awakened at 03:00 a.m. and told that my troop had been selected to advance due west at first light and harass the retreating enemy. To accompany me I had a subaltern of the 5th Royal Horse Artillery as a Forward Observation Officer in his Stuart Mk V1 tank known as a Honey, plus an anti-tank gunner subaltern equipped with a 6 pounder [57mm] anti-tank gun mounted on a portee which as I recall was an adapted 15cwt truck. I was put in charge of the operation. The anti-tank gunner had doubts about the ability of his truck to stay with us as the ground ahead was stony, uneven and difficult. I did not see him again once we had left the start line. The Forward Observation Officer stayed about 50 yards to my right rear throughout the day and fulfilled his function well. We were shelled at intervals including air bursts, uncomfortable for a tank commander who normally functioned with their head out of the turret. With 25 pounder gunfire from the RHA and our tank fire we were able to cause some discomfort to the enemy which was why he shelled us.[12]

Lightly wounded panzer grenadiers just out of action. (Courtesy of H Wernamann)

12 Ibid. H. Limer 1999.

Rommel wrote in his diary:

> Shortly after passing the eastern boundary of our own minefields our troops came up against an extremely strong and hitherto unsuspected British mine belt which was stubbornly defended. Before long relay bombing attacks by the RAF began on the area occupied by our attacking force. With parachute flares turning night into day large formations of aircraft unloosed sticks of high explosive bombs amongst the troops. The army staff spent the night on the telephone with reports pouring in in a continual stream. Even so there remained considerable uncertainty about the situation, although it gradually became clear that things could not have gone altogether as planned. [Quite an understatement][13]

Aerial view of bombs falling on German positions, the tanks and vehicles on the ground can be seen as small black shapes in between the explosions. (Author's collection)

13 B. Liddel-Hart. *The Other Side of the Hill* (London: Pan Books 1983) p. 258.

The night brought no relief for the Axis Forces as the Desert Air Force continued to bomb and strafe the dispersed units, lighting up the desert floor like day with parachute flares and exposing armour and vehicles to the far ranging night fighters and bombers.

The 4th County of London Yeomanry had a grandstand view of the bombing inflicted that night by the Desert Air Force, an anonymous account by a tankman states:

> It was one of the most awe inspiring sights I shall ever see, there were seldom less than 20 flares up in the air at any one time and the whole valley, with its mass of the Afrika Korps stationary vehicles and tanks, was lit up like a huge orange fairyland. All the time red, orange, green and white tracer was darting hither and thither like little 100 mile-an-hour fairies. The huge flash of bombs, which included two 4,000 pound bombs, also inspired the whole thoroughly warlike scene, with little figures silhouetted against their vehicles as they tried to find cover from our bombs. The bombers were so accurate they bombed right up to our minefield, beyond which, 2,000 yards away, was another of our companies.[14]

Trooper H Metcalfe, Queen's Bays, saw the contribution the Desert Air Force made at first hand:

> Through all of this one must never forget the magnificence of the wonderful Desert Air Force, who could forget those 18 Bostons [bombers] flying over us in impeccable formation at regular intervals to drop their deadly load on the enemy. Once again we formed into column of tanks [Honeys], artillery and infantry, and moved south to the Qattara Depression and then west to Himeimat. I peeped over the top of a ridge where hundreds of enemy lorries lay in the valley preparing to move off, in the tanks went. The lorries were laid out in lines like ships at a review. Down the lanes raced the tanks, every piece of armament being used. Lorries were blowing up and burning, the enemy rushing away to find cover. The appearance of enemy tanks forced us to retire. Over 50 lorries were destroyed, many more damaged and of course our usual collection of prisoners. We got back to our own lines well satisfied, to learn that the enemy forces had been repulsed and were retreating.[15]

Lt Harold Limer, 2 Troop, A Squadron, 44th Battalion Royal Tank Regiment, was moved to the western end of Alam Halfa as the light faded and went into action for the first time:

14 Manuscript sent to author by H. Forth Cottingham 1989.
15 Ibid. H. Metcalfe 1995.

A British tank passing a burning panzer. (Author's collection)

> We were moved forward in the fading light and I fired my first two shots of the war at a German Mk 1V tank which had a 75mm gun. I watched as the two puny 2 pounder shots bounced off its armour. As the enemy traversed his gun towards me I rapidly ordered the driver to reverse down the slight slope and watched as a 75mm armour piecing shell hit the ground a few feet to my right. At least I had spoiled his aim.[16]

Being ever cautious Montgomery began moving more troops to the Alam Halfa sector, now he knew Rommel had committed his main force he was determined he should advance no further. 151 [Durham] Brigade of the 50th Northumbrian Division was ordered to cease its work in the Delta and move forward to the eastern end of Alam Halfa Ridge, they were joined on 23rd August by two companies of the 5th Battalion East Yorkshire Regiment who were attached to the 6th Battalion Durham Light Infantry. The brigade was very active from the start and gained valuable experience, the war diary states:

16 Ibid. H. Limer 1999.

> A reconnaissance patrol under Captain Lindrea went out to reconnoitre the area, the patrol came under heavy fire approaching the area and had to dodge a strong enemy patrol on the way out. On the way back one patrol engaged an enemy patrol, believed to be German, 30 yards south of west end of the Jarrow Gap, and had to make a detour through the Don Minefield to get back to our lines. On Captain Lindrea's return a strong fighting patrol was sent out under Lt Lawrence to try to destroy the enemy ambushing party, the enemy had withdrawn. A reconnaissance patrol under Lt Galloway encountered a strong enemy force and was fired on by several machine-guns and mortars.[17]

Montgomery now had Rommel boxed in and in the south the 7th Armoured Division began to make sorties against his flanks. The 9th Australian Division attacked the German 164th Light Division and took many prisoners, this stressed the vulnerability of the Axis Forces that were strung out across the desert and caused alarm among their commanders. The Desert Air Force plagued the Afrika Corps, making sortie after sortie to devastating effect.

Alfons Selmayr, 5th Panzer Regiment, 21st Panzer Division, remembers being on the receiving end of the allied air attacks:

> Now the British Air Force began to have an effect, we had never experienced anything like it before. Without pause they came over us like squadrons at a Nazi Party demonstration and wherever they could see only a few vehicles together they unloaded. My Panzer shook at the seams. A Company commander's tank in front of me received a direct hit on the turret. The commander and loader were badly wounded and died later and the gunner and radio operator were seriously injured. Apart from a few bandages I had no more medical equipment.[18]

By now Rommel knew his offensive had failed. Materials that he had been promised never materialised and he had been held up by a superior force on a ground of their choosing. On 2nd September and with a heavy heart he ordered all formations to withdraw gradually through the gaps in the British minefields to the western edge of these fields of death. Rommel was puzzled by Montgomery's tactics, he knew the British had assembled a powerful armoured force but had kept it in its assembly area. He came to the conclusion that Montgomery was a very cautious man who would never take an unnecessary risk. Montgomery believed that the Eighth Army was not yet ready to take on the task of a possible pursuit and ordered instead that the enemy

17 E.W. Clay. *The Path of the 50th* (Aldershot: Gale and Polden, 1950), p. 189.
18 Manuscript sent to author by H. Wernamann 1987.

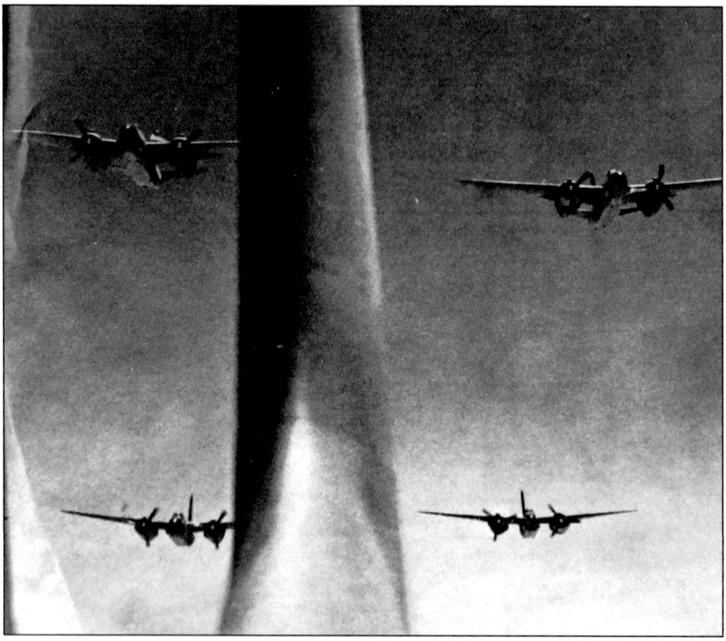

Boston bombers fly in perfect formation as they take the fight to the enemy. Air crew casualties in the Desert Air Force were very high. (Author's collection)

Sappers marking a gap in a minefield. (Courtesy of Norman Hardy)

was to be vigorously harassed. The British then moved forward and began closing the minefield gaps behind the Axis Forces on the night of 3rd September. Diversionary raids were made by the 26th Battalion New Zealanders, the 28th Maori Battalion and 132 Brigade on the night of 3rd September.

Two battalions of 132 Brigade, Royal West Kents, made their approach march under cover of darkness, smoke was laid down by their artillery on the night of 3rd, followed by anti-tank units, tanks and engineers. The first Italian positions were rushed by the British infantry, the surprise and violence of the assault took them completely unawares. As the West Kents overran the forward positions the next line of defence soon brought the Italian paratroopers anti-tank units and mortar teams into action. Blazing vehicles lit up the desert like day exposing the infantry to the gaze of the Italian artillery spotters who brought down a fierce barrage on the British infantry, their close packed columns were perfect targets for the enemy gunners. The advancing British Valentine tanks soon became targets as they approached the Italian line and it was not long before many of them were blazing hulks adding even more light to this already illuminated scene of carnage.

The paratroopers of the Italian Folgore Division met the British with a hail of fire that hampered the advance. Heavy fighting went on throughout the night as the Axis troops tried to prevent the closing of the minefield gaps. At mid-day on 4th September the enemy twice counter-attacked the New Zealanders, each assault being halted by heavy artillery fire and air attacks.

Italian anti-tank gunners in action. (Author's collection)

Lt D Longo, Italian Folgore Parachute Division, was taken by surprise when the assault came in:

> The New Zealand infantry units surprised us and rushed our defences, within a few seconds they were upon us. I saw Sergeant Major Cogoini falling to the ground after being bayoneted in the chest. I witnessed another platoon leader, Sergeant Giovanni, brought down by enemy fire. Then I heard some screams followed by the crackle of machine-gun fire. At this point a number of our sentries jumped out and started back toward our main position to spread the alarm. I then found myself face to face with an enemy fighter as he grabbed me and pushed me to the ground.[19]

Sergeant E. Giacciero, Italian Folgore Parachute Division, was with an anti-tank unit when the first shock of the assault came in:

> I immediately alerted our anti-tank crews and ordered them to start shooting at once. Soon they scored their first direct hit of the night when it pierced an armoured vehicle causing a huge blaze. The fire lit up the battle-field in front of our position and I spotted more than 200 enemy troops in the distance that were in the process of assaulting us with bayonets. Slightly behind this group a number of armoured vehicles were also driving straight at us while firing their machine-guns. Unfortunately in these initial stages most of our crew served weapons, given the commotion, we were not deployed in time and as a result a fierce hand to hand combat ensued.[20]

In the mad melee of the attack and counter attack both sides suffered tremendous numbers killed and wounded. Artillery and mortar fire from both sides swept the area and machine-gun bullets and tracer scythed across the landscape. The fierce reaction of Rommel's forces convinced the New Zealand commander, General Freyberg, that further attacks would not succeed, and he requested permission to withdraw which was granted.

The New Zealanders had lost nearly 1,000 men. The Battle of Alam Halfa ended with Rommel's forces on the western side of the British minefields, he was also left in possession of the high ground at Mount Himeimat in the south, this objective being held by the Italian Folgore Parachute Division in their first baptism of fire. The loss of this high ground was to have serious consequences for XIII Corps in the future.

19 P. Morisi. *The Italian Folgore Parachute Division* (Solihull: Helion and Company, 2016), p. 79.
20 Ibid. p. 79.

A Tommy in a typical well concealed slit trench. (Author's collection)

Monty's subordinates were aghast that their commander had allowed Rommel to occupy the commanding heights of Mount Himeimat in the south. Brigadier Roberts of the 22nd Armoured Brigade could not understand Montgomery's refusal to contest possession of Himeimat:

> I do know that the fact that the Germans had Himeimat was a very severe handicap to us when we came to the main battle of Alamein. And I'm thinking of myself because 7th Armoured Division was in the south and had this bloody Himeimat looking right down on us all the time. If we'd taken Himeimat then it would have eased that. From there one saw a very large amount of the battlefield. It was a tremendously important position and very difficult to get people off it. I think personally it would have been worthwhile having a try and if it seemed difficult then give it up. I don't know how much Monty appreciated that it was a tremendous vantage point looking up the whole of the Alamein line.[21]

21 N. Hamilton. *Monty* (London: Hodder and Stoughton, 1981), p. 84.

Monty appreciated all too well the value of the high ground at Himeimat, though he saw no reason to share this with his subordinates, he surrendered it for a specific purpose, that was to keep Rommel at Alamein in the south on the edge of the Quattara Depression where his lines of communication were stretched to their limits, ensuring that the Axis Forces lines would be too thinly held to repulse a determined British armoured attack delivered at a certain point. If the British generals did not see the reasoning behind Montgomery's strategy it seemed all too obvious to his opponent. Rommel wrote in his diary:

> British ground forces, as has been shown, had hardly put in an appearance during the [German/Italian] offensive. Montgomery had attempted no large scale attack to re-take the southern part of his line and would probably have failed if he had. He had relied instead on the effect of his enormously powerful artillery and air force. Added to this our lines of communication had been subjected to continual harassing attacks by the 7th Armoured Division. There is no doubt that the British commander's handling of this action had been absolutely right and well suited to the occasion, for it had enabled him to inflict very heavy damage on us in relation to his own losses and to retain the striking power of his own force.[22]

Montgomery was satisfied with the outcome at Alam Halfa, he realised that the tactics he had applied proved that his reinforced and rebuilt Eighth Army was more than a match for the Afrika Korps. After Alam Halfa all of Montgomery's energy was focused on his proposed offensive to break Rommel's forces and he applied himself to the preparations needed for the coming struggle.

In the lull that followed Montgomery integrated his new divisions just arrived in Africa with his veteran divisions and they all began to train hard for the coming battle. In October 1942 the British arrayed 11 fighting divisions with four armoured divisions whose tank strength was 1,030, 250 of these being the new heavy Sherman tanks. In support were 530 aircraft and 500 artillery pieces. The Axis Forces had 330 aircraft in support of 500 artillery pieces. But of Rommel's divisions only four were German and the Italian forces did not enjoy his confidence. Early blows and heavy losses had shaken the Italians' commitment to the Axis cause and the entry of America into the war had made them even more uncertain. The Italian troops had a marked lack of motorised transport, a supply situation that was never reliable and were poorly equipped and led, all of these things made them feel like cannon fodder for the Afrika Korps. The Folgore Parachute Division was the exception as they were hard disciplined troops and would prove their worth in the heat of battle.

22 Ibid., p. 85.

A company of the Italian Folgore Parachute Division on parade with mascot. (Author's collection)

Rommel in conversation with some of his commanders at the front. (Courtesy of H. Wernamann)

Rommel was aware that a new British offensive was in the offing and was so unsure of the Italians ability to stand and fight he decided to strengthen his line with German units placed at intervals so that no long section would depend solely on the Italian forces. But Rommel was also troubled by other pressing problems, his army was now overextended and was 1,200 miles from Tripoli, his health was failing fast and by 22nd September 1942 it came to the point where he could carry on no longer and was invalided home to Germany to recuperate. He was replaced by General Stumme, who was a leading exponent of armoured warfare and had been a successful panzer commander in Russia. No doubt he was not sorry to leave that bleak theatre of war for the sun in Africa, though the move would eventually prove fatal for him.

Field Marshall Rommel's Adjutant, Captain Hans Otto Behrendt, recalls Rommel's reaction to the set back at Alam Halfa:

> His was a cool and logical realisation that he had lost the initiative forever. He always called Montgomery the Fox and thought he was a very cautious man. He told me at the end of September 1942 that if he had been as strong as Montgomery is now we wouldn't be standing here.[23]

23 J. Lucas. *Panzer Army Afrika* (London: Purnell Books 1977), p. 126.

3

Attack on the Munassib Depression 30th September–1st October 1942 44th Home Counties Division

During September there was a lull in the fighting and the Axis defences were strengthened and reinforced in preparation for the next round of attacks by the British.

Lt R.J. Jeffery, 44th Reconnaissance Regiment, was in the southern part of the line in late September with the 44th Home Counties Division, his unit was reformed, and he found himself in a new carrier battalion:

> Saw some lively action today when an ME 109 [Messerschmitt], piloted by Unteroffizier Bernhardt Armstadt, disintegrated in mid-air after combat with RAF Tomahawks. The planes' wings fell all around us in small pieces and the main body of the plane hit the ground not 10 yards from Intelligence ARC [armoured car]. We heard the staccato roar of machine-guns and cannon and as it got louder a roaring zoom made us look up. Bartlett shouts 'look out it's dropping something', in a flash I was flat on my face under the ARC with him beside me. I tensed myself for the explosions of bombs which never came, only a muffled thud at 2 or 300 yards as the plane bit the dust. We stood up as all manner of bits and pieces fluttered to earth. Everyone was on the scene hunting for souvenirs. When the excitement died down we buried him [Armstadt] in the afternoon, piled desert rocks high on him, as there's never any soft sand when you want it and a cross now marks the spot. This is war and there is no time for sentiment, we must get on with our jobs.[1]

1 Manuscript sent to author by R.J. Jeffery 1990.

A soldier of the 44th Home Counties Division. (Author's collection)

Troops pose on a shot down Messerschmitt. (Courtesy of Brian Cook, Carnegie Heritage Centre, Hull)

In late September Operation Braganza was planned on XIII Corps front in the south, it was to be led by 131 Brigade, 44th Home Counties Division, and the main objective of it was to capture an area where artillery could be deployed to good effect on the high ground of the Munassib Depression. It would also hold the enemy's attention in the south. Fighter bombers, fighter aircraft and nine field artillery regiments would herald the attack and soften up the enemy positions on this formidable natural fortress. The Italian defences were complimented by extensive barbed-wire entanglements, anti-tank ditches and minefields. Anti-tank and mortar crews were well concealed, each giving the other supporting cross fire.

The British had prepared for days for Operation Braganza and believed, after numerous scouting missions had been completed, that these enemy positions were held by under strength infantry units from the Italian Trieste Division which had been badly mauled at Alam Halfa.

Italian artillery troops prepare to fire. (Author's collection)

The attacking force believed they were going to have an easy time of it, Pte Jack York, 1/5th Battalion the Queens, expected very little trouble:

> Rumour had it that the enemy here consisted of Italian pioneer units and second-rate troops, in which case we were told the attack would be a piece of cake.[2]

2 Letter to author from J. York, Essex 1991.

In fact the whole position was held by the paratroopers of the Italian Folgore Division, a unit known for its tenacity and ability in war. They had developed effective self-supporting defensive positions all over the depression and would be supported by massed artillery situated in the rear areas which could be called upon at any time. In the early hours of September 30th the troops of the 1/5th, 1/6th and 1/7th Battalions of the Queen's Royal West Surrey Regiment began their approach march on foot while their artillery bombarded the enemy positions with high explosive shells. Enemy gun pits and machine-gun posts were blown to pieces in this violent fusillade and the 1/5th Queens led the attack, while the 1/6th and 1/7th Battalions took up supporting positions to their rear. The 1/5th, under cover of a smoke screen, advanced through the enemy wire with the barrage thundering before them. The Italian troops put up flares which enabled them to see the advanced troops of the 1/5th and at once machine-gun and mortar fire fell among the attackers. They had passed an Italian strongpoint and came under fire from front and rear and were cut up badly, those that survived were taken prisoner by the Italian paratroopers who launched a number of determined counter attacks.

Italian anti-tank gun crew pose for the camera. (Author's collection)

Captain Chieppa of the Folgore Division watched the 1/5th Battalion pass by his position:

> When the enemy's artillery barrage ceased we saw six armoured vehicles and numerous infantry units advancing toward us. We allowed these units to advance

> toward the barbed wire by not firing a single shot. Since on our side there had been no reaction the enemy units passed over the wire and into our defensive perimeter. I would venture to say that they advanced deep into our defences probably because they were thinking that we had abandoned our positions. Once they crossed over the wire we all opened fire on them, many of them went to ground and began firing back at us, while the armoured vehicles drove toward us. One of our anti-tank units, which was positioned at a distance of approximately 200 metres from the vehicles, opened fire and immobilised two vehicles. The remaining four vehicles first attempted to bypass our stronghold and then retreated.[3]

Cpl Ernest Norris, 1/5th Queens, 44th Home Counties Division was taken prisoner on that day:

> I don't know by how much, but we were certainly delayed by a lot. The creeping barrage was too far in front of us, but we couldn't change that. We fixed bayonets, formed up in line and were ordered forward, at the time I felt pretty good, proud even. Our barrage was going ahead of us and gave us a feeling of protection, then suddenly the barrage stopped, you feel so naked when that happens you can't describe it. In a matter of seconds they were firing tracer bullets at us, it was still dark, and I was aware of the tracer coming straight toward us, they seemed to be too slow to be bullets. But there were men getting killed and wounded all around, we had passed a number of enemy machine-gun posts that the barrage had missed and were being fired on from behind as well as from the front and there we were literally pinned down. Captain Clarke was mortally wounded, and I heard him call out 'carry on'. Mr Cole-Biroth shouted 'I've been hit' and then my bren-gunner screamed and went down. I then mentally panicked as I didn't know what was happening. By then it was almost daylight and we got down behind what cover we could find. I looked around, Captain Clarke was dead, Mr Cole-Biroth was badly wounded and Mr Whittaker had most of his face shot away. We had no officers left. Being close to the enemy we could hear voices; they came towards us knowing we could not do anything to them. Suddenly they were standing above us shouting and ordering us by signs to take off our equipment and throw our rifles down and come out and that is what we did.[4]

3 P. Morisi, *The Italian Folgore Parachute Division* (Solihull: Helion and Company 2016), p. 95.

4 *Queen's in the Middle East* <www.queensroyalsurreys.org.uk/ww2/middle_east> (Accessed 5 November 2018).

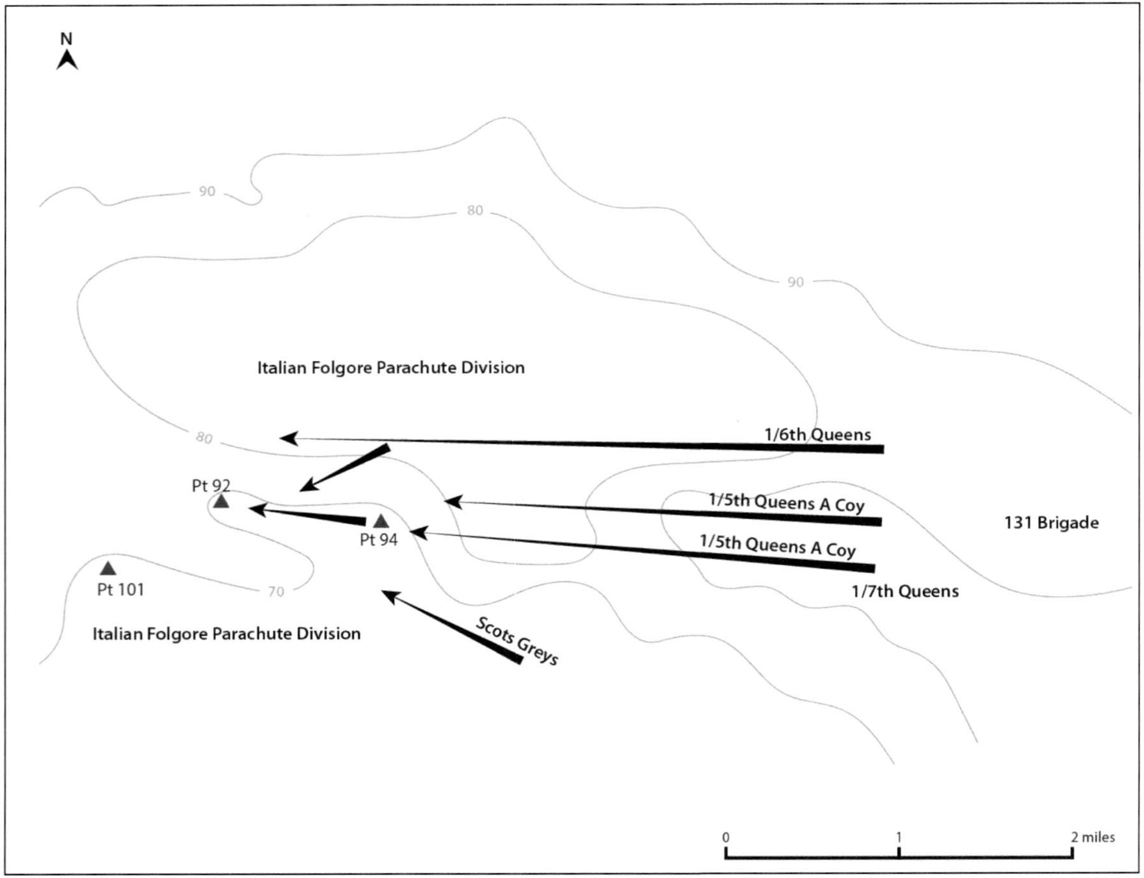

The attack on the Munassib Depression by 44th Home Counties Division, 30th September to 1st October 1942.

Italian troops operating a field radio. (Courtesy of Harry Forth)

Lt Kenneth D Kettle MC, Mortar Platoon Commander, 1/6th Queens, 131st Brigade, recalled a new weapon that they had never experienced before, the Nebelwerfer or multi barrelled rocket launcher:

> The mortars and carriers found great difficulty in the dark, with intermittent shelling from tanks and artillery, in finding cover in support of the forward companies. I was forced to get out of my vehicle to run across areas to find each one of our four sergeants' suitable locations. The noise of our engines together with our tracks over the rocky ground, plus the illumination from our shelling, gave the enemy some idea of the size of our force and position. This invited more direct fire power in the form of the Miniwerfer [Nebelwerfer] it had a barrel like a cement mixer that fired eight sizeable mortar bombs in succession, each with its own hideous whistle that followed its passage before exploding on the ground, adding to the confusion and fear. I will never forget when one of these bombs whistled down suddenly and landed right in front of me in the soft sand with a dull thud. There was no explosion thank God as it was a dud. I didn't dwell and didn't have time to think of the fatal consequences that might have been. In fact I preferred to think that my luck was in, it was a good omen. A sergeant and others told me sometime afterwards [jokingly, I hope] that they were mighty pleased not to have to hang around looking for [my] pieces. At

the approach of dawn my mortar teams were well dug-in to support the leading companies [1/5th Queens] but the forward exposed slope would prevent any movement by day. Towards evening an enemy counter attack could be seen forming up, Major Arthur Richard Trench, MC, the company commander, with complete disregard for his own safety, accompanied by CSM William Richard Stratford, went from platoon to platoon directing the fire of all his weapons, including his medium machine-guns, on the enemy. He and CSM Stratford were hit and died of their wounds later.[5]

Italian troops watching an attack by Stuka dive-bombers on British positions. (Courtesy of H Wernamann)

Italian artillery fire now began to fall on the attacking infantry of the Queens and on the access points to the Munassib Depression, exacting a heavy toll in casualties. The 131st Brigade had suffered well over 300 dead, wounded and taken prisoner. The Folgore Division had lost only 45 other ranks and six officers. Throughout the assault on Munassib the 21st Panzer Division was stationed in the rear of the Folgore Division in case of a breakthrough by the British, the fact that they were not deployed is a tribute to the troops defending the position and precious tanks were preserved to fight another day.

5 *BBC World War II Peoples War Stories* <bbc.co.uk/history/ww2peopleswar/stories> (Accessed 12th October 2017).

Brigadier Frith, C/O 131st Brigade, intended to resume the attack later on 1st October but there were delays and confusion in the preparation. The Corps Commander, General Horrocks, called the operation off. The ground that had been gained by the British infantry at a terrible cost in lives was later occupied on 1st October by 132 Brigade, 44th Home Counties Division. The main causes of the failure of the attack was said to be that most of the artillery supporting fire was wasted because of faulty intelligence regarding the make-up and dispositions of the enemy forces, the rough ground over which the infantry had to advance and the relative inexperience of the attacking troops. The troops of the Italian Folgore Parachute Division, although vastly outnumbered, had proved themselves to be capable and aggressive soldiers in battle and would continue to do so throughout the campaign. Coming as it did before Montgomery's main effort at Alamein the attack on Munassib has received little attention, but without doubt it influenced his tactics for Operation Lightfoot.

4

Preparations for Second Alamein October 1942

Montgomery's planned October offensive had been conceived by him in an altogether different style from anything that had gone before, his predecessors had been lured into using their tanks as a principal tactical instrument. The freedom of manoeuvre offered by the desert terrain had proved too tempting but the hopes of implementing a panzer style Blitzkrieg had never materialised. Three times before the enemy had been chased out of their positions back to Tripoli, Montgomery had grave doubts about the ability of his armoured divisions to outwit the Germans. His new plan was for a set piece battle that would inflict on the Axis Forces a crushing defeat from which they would not recover.

Allied air power had increased dramatically by October 1942 and the newly arrived crews of the B-25 Mitchells and Wellingtons began to train in their role as long range bombers that was to play such a major part of the tactical planning for the coming desert offensive. Pilot officer Harry Hawker served with 208 Squadron, Royal Desert Air Force:

> We were doing visual reconnaissance over the Alamein Line at about 4,000 feet, which was a bad height as we were shot at by light flak and heavy flak from the 88s. Each recce consisted of the pilot doing the recce and someone else weaving behind him to protect his tail. As you flew over the Line you couldn't see much if they were well camouflaged, what we were looking for was movement and the dust it caused. You had to be quick in assessing numbers, so if you saw a bunch of trucks or tanks you would have to say something like 25 plus. You always flew with the hood open because the visibility was so poor through the crazed plexiglas. The German flak was accurate, but we weaved so casualties were not high. Casualties from fighters was much higher, I was lucky only to have seen enemy fighters, but not to have been attacked by them, because they had about a 50 percent success rate against us. The enemy 109 [Messerschmitt] would get very high and go for us in a steep dive going

Men of the Royal Tank Regiment use a lull in the fighting to overhaul their Honey light tank. (Author's collection)

Kittyhawk fighters of the Desert Air Force out on patrol searching for the enemy. (Author's collection)

> very fast, so time to pick him up was short and he would belt you with a short burst. If the weaver saw him he would call out and turn to attack, if he could get round in time you had a good chance of spoiling his afternoon. We lost 21 pilots in 19 days on this activity over Alamein.[1]

The improvement for the Eighth Army in allied air and sea power in the Mediterranean ensured an ever increasing volume of supplies. The Axis Forces however now experienced a considerable reduction in the supply of arms and fuel for the same reasons. The great battle of Alamein, which was planned to begin in October's full moon, was to be a deliberate infantry and artillery assault supported by tanks. Only after this first stage, or as Monty called it 'The dog fight' would the bulk of the armour be launched. The infantry battalions would be first to cross the as yet unknown hazards of no-man's land and in the dust and smoke suffer the fusillade of machine-gun fire from the enemy out-post line. Their slow paced advance would take them through the enemy's main minefields where the danger of death and mutilation would be ever present. In the process they would encounter furious opposition as defensive artillery barrages came down upon them combined with heavy concentrations of machine-gun fire, rifle fire and mortar fire, all working in unison to break the attack.

A Honey tank at Alamein passing a rocky escarpment. (Author's collection)

Montgomery now began a period of intense training and preparation for all his forces, to instil confidence in his men and their commanders he visited units regularly and took the officers into his confidence. It was not sufficient to order men to attack at a certain place at a certain time, Montgomery wanted to foster a feeling among all ranks

1 Manuscript sent to author by Peter Wing 1994.

that they were trusted comrades taking part in momentous events. This was much appreciated by all ranks. Lt Scotty White of the 9th Battalion Durham Light Infantry recalled the effect of one of these visits:

> One of Monty's qualities was the way he transmitted his intention to the army, to blokes like me right down at the lower end, the way he inspired confidence and that things would go the way he said they would. Some couldn't care less what they heard, but allowing for that element, everybody was raring to go.[2]

Cpt Peter Lewis, 8th Battalion Durham Light Infantry, had similar feelings:

> Our CO went for a briefing of all COs by Monty and he passed it on to us. Monty said there would be a dog fight for 10 days. He explained how the battle would be fought and was confident of the result. When we were told this all leave was cancelled, there was a tremendous state of enthusiasm and morale was terrific. We had never had an army commander who gave us such a message. Our chaps were pretty good and will do what they are told and do it even better when they know what they are supposed to be doing.[3]

Panzer Grenadiers relax during a lull in the fighting. (By courtesy of Harry Forth)

2 H. Moses. *The Gateshead Gurkhas* (Durham: County Durham Books, 2001), p. 96.
3 Manuscript sent to author by Ian R English. Durham 1990.

Trooper Eric Alsop of the Royal Tank Regiment found it a refreshing change when the old tactics of the tank commanders were dumped, and a more disciplined approach was being enforced in no uncertain terms:

> They were to get the idea at last and they were not going to swan about the battle-field in columns. No more fluid this and that, going around the back of them and all that stuff. Monty said we are going to fight in divisions as we are trained to fight. The tanks were well sited and told you are not going back. Rommel was very unpleasantly surprised.[4]

Cpl Peter Roach, 1st Battalion Royal Tank Regiment, 7th Armoured Division, thought it nothing short of miraculous that the men were being told of what was happening:

> The mood had changed from chagrined defeat and humiliation to a hard confidence tinged with wonder. Then miracles of miracles we paraded and were told the outlines of the battle to come. This was genius. Our primary task was to simulate an attack in the south drawing in the Italian divisions without transport further into the desert. The main breakthrough would be in the north. General Montgomery's orders were read out, his stilted cricketing metaphors accepted by this irreverent bunch of military pirates.[5]

In August 1942 Churchill addressed troops on a hot sweltering day in the desert, giving them an inkling that great things were afoot:

> Gentlemen, you will strike an unforgettable blow against the enemy. The corn will be ripe for the sickle and you will be the reapers, may God bless you all.[6]

4 Letter to author Eric Alsop 1994.
5 Ibid., Peter Roach 1991.
6 C.E. Lucas, *Alamein* (London. Heinemann, 1962) p. 244.

5

Operation Lightfoot Role of XXX Corps and XIII Corps

The front-line at Alamein was held by two infantry corps with the armoured corps to their rear. To the north was XXX Corps, whose principal task was the creation of gaps through the minefields, through these would pass the tanks of X Corps. In the south XIII Corps would mount a series of diversionary attacks with the intention of holding two Axis armoured divisions in the southern part of the line and prevent them from moving north to attack XXX Corps. The XIII Corps was also to make minefield gaps so that when the Axis Forces started to retreat the British armour in that sector had a path through which it could strike and cut off Rommel's defeated forces. While the engineers of XXX Corps in the north were clearing gaps in the minefields the infantry would advance to secure a bridge-head beyond the Axis first line positions on the western side of Miteiriya Ridge. The British armour could then leap frog through the infantry once their positions had been consolidated, this, if carried out successfully, would mark the end of the break-in stage of Operation Lightfoot. A name of great significance for the infantry and the engineers who would have to walk through fields sown with thousands of mines.

XXX Corps

In the northern coastal sector on the right wing of XXX Corps was the 9th Australian Division. It was their task to storm the enemy positions from their present sector at Tel el Eisa, to move westward across no-man's land and carry on some 6,000 yards to a line on the map known as Oxalic. To their left was the 51st Highland Division whose task it was to advance across the desert and form the northern corridor through the enemy minefields, their final objective was a line on the map known as the Blue Line. To the left of the Highland Division were the New Zealanders who were seriously short of infantry, their present establishment being only two brigades. They were reinforced by the 9th Armoured Brigade to increase their fire power and to enable them to be successful in their given task. The 2nd New Zealand Division were to advance on a south westerly line and capture the north western section of Miteiriya Ridge. On their

British troops inspect a knocked out 88mm gun and its half-track. (Courtesy of Ralph Hymer)

A soldier of the DLI shaves in a quiet moment. (Author's collection)

left flank was the 1st South African Division who were fortunate in that their advance had to travel only 5,000 yards to its final objective. The last division on the left flank of XXX Corps was positioned around Ruweisat Ridge, this was the 4th Indian Division, one of the most experienced divisions in the line. However their task for Operation Lightfoot was to be a purely diversionary role. To the rear of these infantry divisions was X Corps consisting of the 1st and 10th Armoured Divisions.

XIII Corps

South of Ruweisat Ridge and on the left flank of the 4th Indian Division was XIII Corps, their line stretched to the south as far as the unforgiving features of Mount Himeimat. On the right flank stood the 1st Greek Brigade, commanded by Lt Colonel Katssotos, these men were tough fighters, dedicated patrollers and collectors of Italian ears, they replaced 150 Brigade that had been lost at Gazala and were now under the command of the 50th Division. To their left sat 151 Durham Brigade and 69 Brigade of the 50th Northumbrian Division, they proudly wore the distinctive TT shoulder flash [Tyne Tees] and like the 51st Highland Division and the 7th Armoured Division was another of the great fighting divisions that Montgomery took with him wherever he went, using them in one major assault after another in Africa, Sicily, Normandy and after.

Montgomery addresses the Greek Minister of Defence, Panagiotis Kanelopoulos, as he fixes the badge of 1st Greek Brigade to his cap. (From the Captain S. Tzanetis archive, courtesy of Stefanos Moraitis of Greece)

The infantry of the 50th Division came mainly from Durham and Yorkshire, the Durham Brigade and the Rhodesian Anti-tank gunners of the 50th would soon find themselves sent north to help the Australians and New Zealanders in Operation Supercharge. On the left flank of the 50th Division, holding a long front, consisting of rough ground and soft sand, stood the division that had the hardest luck of all. This was the 44th Home Counties Division, which had formerly been commanded by Brian Horrocks and was commanded now by Ivor Hughes. Its troops were drawn mainly from Kent, Surrey and Sussex and it had suffered heavy casualties at Alam Halfa and before, two of its brigades would be taken away to provide lorried infantry for the 7th and 10th Armoured Divisions. The 44th would be broken up shortly after Alamein. To their rear was the 7th Armoured Division which was stationed in the soft sand of the Ragil Depression and commanded by General Harding. The 7th had no infantry brigade and mechanically its tanks and wheeled transport was in a run-down condition, it had no Shermans and its strongest brigade, 22nd Armoured Brigade, had 126 tanks of various kinds. The 4th Light Brigade was down to 81 tanks but possessed 170 armoured cars, enabling them to patrol the enormous no-man's land that stretched five miles between the opposing minefields. The extreme left flank of XIII Corps was held by the 2nd Free French Brigade and commanded by General Marie Pierre Koenig. The ground here under the shadow of Mount Himeimat was difficult and these Frenchmen were the heroes of Bir Hacheim, where they had made an epic stand against Rommel's forces in the Gazala Line. They were a mix of French Legionnaires and colonial troops and were under the command of the 7th Armoured Division.

General Marie Pierre Koenig. CO 2nd Free French Brigade. (Author's collection)

The 50th Division prepared for the fight to come under the command of General John Sebastian Nichols, [nick-named Crasher] DSO, MC. The Divisional HQ was visited by an American contingent of senior officers in early October, Lt Colonel Beowold Innes, GSO 1, recalled the occasion:

> Crasher's place was on the battle-field where things were hottest, and it was this predilection for fighting that was eventually to prove his undoing as a divisional commander. Nevertheless he set an unrivalled example to all ranks by his determination to be with his men where the bullets were flying. He had the reputation of being bullet-proof, but anyone who saw him disrobe for his morning jerks had visible evidence that a great many bullets had passed through him without much effect. I often recall the following incident at Alamein, two American Colonels had been sent to us to see how a divisional battle was run. They were both prospective GSO1s, or whatever they are called in US Divisions. They sure thought they were tough and they seemed to be of considerable antiquity and old enough to be my father. They reminded me of the types you see in westerns, chewing cigars and shooting the sheriff. On arrival they looked scornfully around Divisional HQ and said they had come to see the boys in battle not a bunch of Limey generals. Crasher told them that next day he personally would put them in the picture. Next day they had breakfast and departed to see how the British Army did things. In the evening the party returned, Crasher, spritely as ever, waddled off to his caravan wiggling the cane he always carried. Not so the Americans, when Crasher had gone one of them leant on my shoulder and said 'Colonel, lead me to a high ball and make it a strong one, that General of yours sure goes places and likes to see the sparks fly'. He kept them going places for the whole week and they left with a very different picture of a modern British General.[1]

The first task for XIII Corps in the south was to smash through the enemy defences at their weakest point between the Munasib Depression and Mount Himeimat. The object would be to draw the enemy armoured reserve to the south. The enemy positions in the south were protected by deep belts of minefields and the unenviable task of clearing a way through them was given to the 44th Home Counties Division who were to secure a bridgehead, as soon as it had been secured the 7th Armoured Division would pass through and turn north to roll up the enemy line in rear of the Munassib sector. While this was being done the 50th Division was to make a frontal attack east and north of the Munassib Depression, advancing over 1,000 yards from its start line. The Corps Commander decided that the 50th Division would make its

1 Manuscript sent to author by the wife of Colonel Beowold Innes 1989.

General John Sebastian Nichols, DSO, MC. OC 50th Northumbrian Division. (Author's collection)

move on the night subsequent to the assault by the 44th Home Counties Division and not before the 7th Armoured Division had succeeded in outflanking the enemy troops facing the division.

In the weeks before 23rd October the 44th Home Counties Division played an important role in Operation Bertram, this was a deception plan intended to persuade the enemy that large numbers of troops, vehicles and armour had been moved to the southern sector in preparation for a major offensive there. Day after day whole battalions from the 44th were carried to the rear by night and brought back in daylight, giving the Italian and German observers on Himeimat the impression that large numbers of infantry were moving to the southern front. To the rear of the 44th Division numerous dummy tanks and vehicles stood in the desert in full view of any enemy aircraft that flew over.

Lt G. Raphael took part in the deception plan:

> I was a Lt in 1509th [Seychelles] Pioneer Company. We were engaged in creating a concourse of tanks and lorries and even a HQ to confuse enemy reconnaissance planes, it was done with hessian, some string and some very light wooden poles etc. The dummy camp and vehicle sites were erected at

A blow up dummy rubber tank being carried into position. (Author's collection)

German armour and a medical unit watch a bombardment from a distance. (Courtesy of Max Hearst)

> night with the help of moonlight and during daylight gave the appearance of busy military areas to the very high flying enemy planes. Vehicles travelled around and about creating clouds of dust and in the early morning every encouragement to brewing up in amongst the dummy bivouacs was given, and of course around the vehicles or tanks outlined in hessian and supported by thin wooden poles and cats cradles of strong twine. General Stone and a Brigadier arrived just before noon on 15th October and saw the erection of dummy tanks and vehicles and seemed duly impressed.[2]

Lt Brian [Barney] O'Kelly, Intelligence Corps:

> Down south in X111 Corps we were the decoy. A dummy pipe-line had been laid forward to us, AFVs [armoured fighting vehicles] were concentrated in the area, masses of pole and canvas mock-up three tonners were assembled and after a night of wind and rain hurriedly straightened up. Extensive dummy WT [wireless traffic] was passed and in general everything was done to convince all branches of the enemy's intelligence that the Eighth Army was intending a left hook attack, driving from the Quattara Depression end of the line and then swinging northwards.[3]

The troops of 69 Brigade, 50th Division, were to assault the Munassib Depression with artillery support. In the depression was a strongly defended island known as the Moor and a plateau come strong point south of the depression with the code name of The Cape. Once these positions had been taken the second objective for the attacking troops was a line of defences 300 yards to the rear of these positions. The assault troops were to be the 6th Battalion Green Howards on the right and the 5th Battalion East Yorkshire Regiment on the left.

The 151st Brigade had a more complicated task they were to push forward one battalion silently during the night and take up positions on the plateau to the north of the Munassib Depression and east of the main enemy defensive minefields. If they occupied this plateau they would be able to dominate the depression when dawn broke. Another battalion would stand by at dawn to mop up any enemy posts on the north side of the depression in cooperation with 69 Brigade. Two field regiments of the Royal Artillery would be on call to assist. On the right of the 50th the 1st Greek Brigade had no actual part in the attack but was to make raids with a view to tying down the German troops to their front and prevent the movement of reserves. If these attacks were successful the 50th would then hold these positions as a firm base

2 Letter sent to author by G Raphael. 1993.
3 Ibid. B O'Kelly. 1991.

A view of the daunting terrain of the Munassib Depression. (Author's collection)

for future operations by XIII Corps, such was the role of the 50th Division in the coming battle.

The whole area occupied by the 50th Division was overlooked by the enemy from Mount Himeimat which stood 700 feet high, causing problems when the movement of men and materials was needed once battle was joined. On the night of 22nd October 1942 the men of the 50th Division settled down to get what rest they could, when the sun dipped below the horizon a great relief was felt as the hard baked ground began to cool as a nightly breeze arose and the ever present hordes of flies gave up their torment. Once more it was possible to move freely around without being visible to the enemy. On the evening of the 23rd a full moon shone, and the desert was still, but in the ranks of a now confident Eighth Army there was an air of suspense. In the four months that had elapsed since the weary troops of the Eighth Army had left the Gazala Line and arrived at the defences of the Alamein Line, great changes had taken place and a new spirit animated the army.

On the morning of Friday 23rd October 1942 the dawn broke cold and clear to herald a bright and sunny day, the sun moved slowly out of the east passing overhead at noon. During the afternoon it began to set behind the German and Italian Lines.

Eighth Army troops in the forward areas looking across no-man's land. (Author's collection)

Cpl William Francis Vickers MM, 6th Battalion Green Howards remembers that day well:

> We knew something big was coming, that evening the sun was a great red ball hanging in the sky and as the last light faded a Khamseen blew for a short while, when it stopped it revealed a bright starlit night and in the silence I thought of home and wondered what were the chances of my survival. A full-moon lit up the landscape and as we sat in full battle gear all was still.[4]

4 Interview with author, William Frances Vickers. 1991.

6

The Battle Begins 23rd October 1942

Along the length of the Alamein Line men were looking at their watches as 21:40 p.m. zero hour, drew closer. Nothing now could stop the operation and the events that were to turn this ordinary day of 23rd October 1942 into a date forever famous in British military history.

As the light fades on the night of 23rd October Sappers await the order to move off. (Courtesy of Charles Spandler)

As the second hands of hundreds of watches registered 21:40 p.m. exactly the order was shouted out in unison from hundreds of throats: Fire! In a thunder of gunfire from the British rear the barrage opened up and the whole front erupted into a single flame as the gunners loaded and fired again and again. The sight and sound of that great barrage would never be forgotten.

Pte Charles Spandler of the Royal Army Service Corps was making a delivery to a forward ammunition dump when it began:

> Just before the firing started we were about a couple of miles in front of the guns at a depot. The Corporal came up to us and said 'I think we'd better get bedded down for the night' and for some unknown reason a hush fell, it was as if a voice shouted three, two, one, quiet everybody. There was a stillness even though people were still moving about. The next thing that we heard there was going to be a barrage and everybody had to be well clear of the perimeter. They opened out with a big flash that lit up the sky, it frightened the hell out of us, it was uncanny. You were deaf to the things around you and there was just the booming of the guns. The whole night was just lit up, even in daylight there was still this awesome flashing as the barrage continued. We stood around in groups that night watching, it's something we'll never see again.[1]

Pte Charles Spandler.
Royal Army Service Corps.
(Courtesy of C Spandler)

1 Interview with author, Charles Spandler Hull 1992.

Pte Harry Forth, 5th Battalion East Yorkshire Regiment, was shaken by the violence of the bombardment:

> Christ it was a hell of a do that one, you've never seen gunfire like it in your life, it was terrifying and you could read a newspaper by its light that night. When you looked across no-man's land at the Gerry lines it was as though they were on fire, the ground looked as though it was boiling. We had no love for Gerry but I felt sorry for him that night. I've never seen anything like it in my life and never wish to see anything like it again. It frightened you even though you knew you were safe.[2]

Sergeant W J Giddings, 5th Battalion Royal Sussex Regiment, was in an advanced position before the balloon went up:

> This officer said to me 'keep looking behind you sergeant, you will see a sight you will never experience again' I kept looking but could see nothing but darkness, so I wondered what the hell he was on about. But at 21:40 p.m. I looked behind me again and it looked as though the whole horizon was on fire. Then there was a few seconds silence and then the sound of whistling in the air above us, followed by the crump of shells exploding on the German lines. The Battle of El Alamein had started, the officer said 'bring your men in sergeant, let's go home.[3]

Lt Colonel William I Watson, 6th DLI:

> The whole night sky to the east was broken by hundreds of gun flashes stabbing into the darkness. The shells whistled and screamed overhead to burst with a deafening crash in the target area and from then, until the barrage closed about three hours later, the frightful shattering noise went on continually.[4]

Lt Harold Limer, 2 Troop, A Squadron, 44th Battalion Royal Tank Regiment, was 200 yards from a 25 pounder gun position at 21:40 a.m. when the barrage opened up:

> It was truly an awesome sight and the vibration made my 16 ton tank rock gently on its suspension as we waited to advance. I had an Aussie soldier on my tank who would lead me to the infantry we were to support. As we moved

2 Ibid. Harry Forth, Cottingham 1991.
3 Manuscript sent to author by W.J. Giddings 1987.
4 Manuscript sent to author by William Ridley Durham 1992.

British artillery firing on the night of 23rd October 1942. (Courtesy of Charles Spandler)

Lt Colonel William Innes Watson, 6th Battalion Durham Light Infantry. (Courtesy of William Ridley)

Wellington bombers fly in formation as they bomb the enemy rear areas and supply lines. (Author's collection)

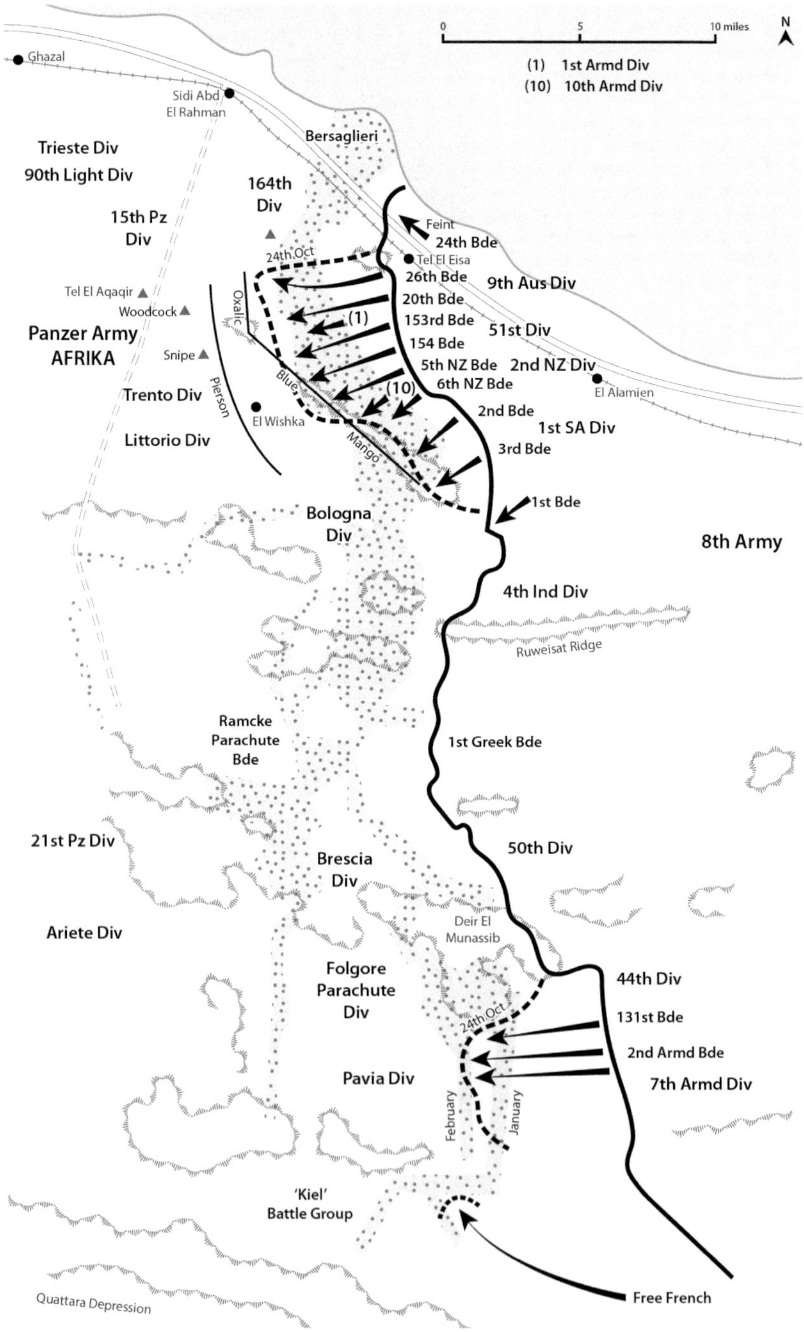

El Alamein, 23rd October 1942.

> off he said, 'take me back to Melbourne' to which I could only reply 'take me back to London'. When the enemy artillery fire landed around us he said, 'I'm off' and I never saw him again. One could not blame him as tank noise attracts a lot of shell-fire and sitting on the outside of a tank was not healthy. There were shouts from the infantry on the ground saying we were too close to their slit trenches, but in the dark and with the noise, dust and confusion it was impossible to see them.[5]

The Axis Forces were completely unprepared for the force of the attack as a total of 592 allied guns opened up simultaneously from the Mediterranean in the north to the Quattara Depression in the south, 456 of them in the northern sector.

Gunner Ranft was with the 164th German Light Division and was on the receiving end of the British barrage:

> On 23rd October at nine o'clock in the evening we thought the world was coming to an end. We got a terrible artillery bombardment from the British, I was in a hole sheltering and was talking to a comrade about bygone days. The whole front line sky went red and he said, 'look at that'. When it started it was horrible, I could hear shells howling over me and we thought that this was the end, but we survived. We were in a hole about one and a half foot deep and when a shell came you knew when it was coming towards you and we sheltered all night long. At times the barrage moved away from where we were, they concentrated on certain areas. We had a quick look out and the ground looked like a ploughed field, there wasn't much left. We thought how can anyone survive this, but we did. We had some casualties but the infantry ahead of us had more. One of my friends had his foot blown off by a shell, he died the next day. One man took a direct hit on the bunker he was in and one shell went right through and blew his head off.[6]

Pilot Officer Ron Dorey was flying his Wellington Bomber over the Alamein Line on the night of 23rd and had no idea what he was about to witness:

> We didn't know that the battle was about to start, I have never seen anything like it, 30 miles of solid gun-fire at night, from the coast to the Quattara Depression. We said, 'bloody hell what's going on?' We thought it was flak at first but as we got nearer we realised what it was and flew over the top, we'd been told not to fly below 6,000 feet. They wanted us to fly up and down the Gerry

5 Ibid. H Limer 1999.
6 Ibid. H. Wernamann, Germany 1989.

British 25 pounder gun team in action. (Courtesy of Jack Verity)

> front line and if we saw flashes to bomb them, a bit ridiculous at that height. So having tried this out the air gunners began to get impatient and wanted me to go lower so they could shoot at the enemy flashes. I said that 6,000 feet was to keep us above our own artillery shells, they said 'go on have a go' so we went back to the coast and hurtled back down the line at 200 feet, the gunners blazed away at the enemy and I don't know if we hit anything. When we got back for debriefing a wing commander was going absolutely spare at another crew on the next table. They had done the same as us, machine-gunning, and unfortunately had got an artillery shell right through the fuselage, in one side and out the other, that was proof of the strength of the Wellington Bomber. Luckily the shell didn't take out the control rods or explode on contact.[7]

The infantry attack by XXX Corps in the north was launched at 22:00 p.m. and had a successful start as the sappers moved forward with their mine detectors and began clearing lanes for the armour. But the depth and density of the mine fields proved a greater obstacle than had been expected and took longer than planned to clear.

Trooper John Lanes was a radio operator in a Sherman tank of the Nottinghamshire Yeomanry, Sherwood Rangers, and saw the effects of the devastating 88 fire on tanks as his unit tried to press through the gaps:

7 J Thompson. *Desert Victory* (London: Ebury Press, 2012] p. 241.

The battle-field grave of a British tank crew next to their knocked-out Sherman. (Author's collection)

> As we moved in front of the guns it was dark and the mines had been lifted by New Zealand sappers. The enemy anti-tank shells had tracer in the base and there was a lot of dust, even so you could see the tracer of the 88 rounds flashing past us. A lot of our tanks got hit but we got through the minefield, however without support we had to turn back.[8]

Lt Harold Limer, 2 Troop, A Squadron, 44th Battalion Royal Tank Regiment, waited in his tank for the move forward through the minefield gaps when he came under friendly fire:

> Bofors anti-aircraft guns were firing tracer at intervals to assist direction finding for the advancing troops and that was very useful in the murk and the all-pervading dust. It was a long very difficult night with tanks nose to tail in the confined space waiting for cleared gaps in the minefields. The sappers were

8 Letter to author from J. Lanes 1989.

doing heroic work in extremely difficult circumstances, but we were well behind schedule and could not marry-up with our infantry until we got through the minefields. The Royal Military Police also performed their traffic control tasks in sterling fashion, as though they were on an exercise. Our soldiers that night formed a different and much higher opinion of the redcaps. Eventually, after much frustration and much reconnoitring on foot, just after first light, we got through the minefields and number 2 Troop turned left to take up our position as the left hand troop of the squadron with Bill Mailley [number 3 Troop] on my right. He moved on to a small crest together with one of his other tanks and both were instantly knocked out by an anti-tank gun. He and the other tank commander were killed and were not able to fire a shot. We were in the former enemy FDLs [Forward Defensive Localities] which the Aussies had taken when 18 Boston Bombers, who we called the Australian Football Team, flew overhead at a great height and dropped their bombs. Unfortunately we got the lot, one fortunately empty bren carrier looked like the proverbial Sieve afterwards, they hit the former FDLs alright but by then we were there.[9]

A German 88 anti-tank gun firing across the battle-field, smoke from hit and burning British tanks can be seen in the distance. (Author's collection)

When daylight came the British armour was still situated within the lanes or just beyond. In the south, XIII Corps prepared to play their part in the battle.

9 Manuscript sent to author by H. Limer 1999.

7

Battle in the South
The 44th Home Counties Division and 7th Armoured Division Attacks 23rd –26th October 1942

The 44th Home Counties Division was in position on the night of the 23rd October and was to make their attack three and a half miles north of Mount Himeimat, 131 Brigade consisted of the 1/5th, 1/6th and 1/7th Battalions of the Queen's Regiment. The 1/7th Queens were now put under the command of the 7th Armoured Division for the operation and moved forward to their assembly area as zero hour approached, walking through the gaps in our own minefields and over the long expanse of No-Man's Land in bright moonlight to their start line. Close behind them came a formidable minefield task force commanded by Lt Colonel L Corbet-Winder, it consisted of Royal Engineers, six Scorpion Tanks fitted with flails, a squadron of armoured cars, two companies of the 1st Rifle Brigade and the 44th Reconnaissance Regiment. Behind the task force came the 22nd Armoured Brigade and the 4th Light Armoured Brigade, each with its own battalion of mortorised infantry, waiting for their opportunity to move forward.

Lt Leslie R. Symonds, 44th Reconnaissance Regiment, remembers the move forward just before the barrage opened:

> We all began to move forward, long columns going back as far as the horizon and beyond, all moving slowly forward. Darkness falls but the huge moon provides an amazing amount of light on this fantastic scene of these columns moving across the desert. Occasionally we are halted, but for hour after hour we move nearer the battle area. Seven, eight, nine o'clock we are still moving forward, but at last we stop. I look ahead at the three vehicles in front and then I look back at the countless vehicles behind. I dish out the rum, great gulping mouthfuls of liquid fire. Our watch hands seem to be moving very slowly as we

Men of The Queen's Regiment, 44th Home Countiies Division. (Author's collection)

Troops of the Queen's regiment move to the start line. (Author's collection)

wait, sweating a little but still cold at the same time. Now suddenly, as though a single button has been pressed, the whole sky behind us is a blaze of light with the flashes from hundreds of guns. A long whining scream overhead and then the desert in front convulses into miniature earthquakes, it is stupendous. Can anything live through that? It can live alright. There are a few minutes of non-retaliation as though the enemy cannot believe it, then a very light goes up, dimming for a moment the flash of shells and suddenly shells are bursting around us. At first I feel nauseating fear, but it goes almost immediately. Those shells are not aimed at me personally and only an unlucky one will hit us. I stand up and look back at the lads, a shell swishes overhead and a carrier in the column on our right receives a direct hit, it was Lt Ronny [Frank Royston] Brinnicombe's vehicle, he and one of his crew were killed outright, the driver was alive with both legs off at the knees. I jumped out of the truck and the lads drop down beside me, they are obviously scared. We pass one, two, three vehicles and here is the hole in the wire marking the first minefield [January], the anti-mine tanks [Scorpions] are already moving forward, the REs are ready and off we go.[1]

Officers of the 1/6th Queens Regiment. (Author's collection)

1 Manuscript sent to author by T.A. Lombard Chester 1991.

Brigadier Pip Roberts of the 7th Armoured Division recalls the accurate enemy fire as the armour approached the January minefield:

> It took a little time to locate the eastern edge of January minefield and by that time the engineers had started the gapping operation, this brought down a heavy enemy concentration of artillery, mortar and machine-gun fire. The Scorpions were continually breaking down through overheating and when mines were cleared, sometimes by hand, vehicles got stuck and could not get forward. The two southern gaps proved the most difficult because of soft sand. The most menacing fire was coming from the left flank from the towering Himeimat. I urged 5th RTR to get through number two gap, then to prepare to move south. Part of the [Scots] Greys were already through and moving south.[2]

British tanks at Alamein. (Author's collection)

Unlike the attacking troops in the north, the infantry in the south came under heavy fire from the start. The 1/7th Queens were being shelled before they left their start line and it was not long before machine-gun and mortar fire began to thin out their ranks. Major Erick William Stillwell, second in command, and two other officers were killed as they set off, plus numerous other ranks. The guns of four field regiments gave supporting fire and as the Queen's progressed shells screamed over their heads exploding with earth shaking detonations on the enemy positions throwing up clouds of dust and smoke.

2 P. Delaforce, *Churchill's Desert Rats* (Stroud: Sutton Publishing, 2002), p. 119.

Their first objective, a minefield 350 yards deep, code named January, was reached and small numbers of men managed to advance to their final objective, a minefield over 1,000 yards deep, code named February. The distance between the two minefields that the infantry would have to walk over was two miles. Many of them were taken prisoner as the Italian paratroopers counter-attacked and the Commanding Officer, Lt Colonel Roderick Montague Burton, was killed trying to escape. The survivors drew back to a wadi at 03:00 a.m. and reformed under the command of Captain P R H Kealy, they took up positions at the head of the newly made minefield gaps in the January minefield.

Sappers await the order to move forward. (Author's collection)

Lt R J Jeffery, 44th Reconnaissance Regiment, moved forward with his carriers as part of the 22nd Armoured Brigade, 7th Armoured Division:

> We were in march positions, Grant tanks are in our column as we plod ahead quietly, slowly but relentlessly covering the ground between us and the first enemy minefield [January]. We have lost the track and turn sharp right in a hasty attempt to retrieve our lost position and catch up on our timetable, we accomplish this quite well, coming up on the left of a long thin column. By this time the distant shelling had become a present and local hazard. Shells were

> falling to our right as we proceeded, and one made a direct hit on a truck which went up in flames. When we reached the minefield Gerry had his guns laid and was expecting an attack. The ridge in front of the minefield he plastered with evil intent and to his good purpose. The air was full of cordite fumes and a smoke pall lay heavily as the squadrons pushed forward to their preliminary jobs of making gaps in the first minefield. Artillery was furiously pasting us now as we lined up patiently on the ridge before the intended gaps and the anti-tank and artillery fire from the other side battered away incessantly at us as we lined up. Three carriers were put out of action on number four gap however progress was made, and the REs suffered severe casualties as a result of machine-gun and mortar fire. There were constant demands on the radio for more reserves who, when they arrived, were immediately sent to help widen and clear the gaps. After a while it became apparent that the obstacles immediately in our path were machine-gun pockets which were causing devastation to the REs. The carefully prepared and practised code of communication was quickly discarded in the heat of action, several times a breathless Major Nesbitt spoke on the air of heavy machine-gun and anti-tank fire, the staccato roar of machine-gun fire in the background. Several times C Squadron asked for our barrage to be raised so that the men could proceed as it was still falling in front of us. The information was radioed back to RAHQ without apparent effect. At last gaps two and three are declared open, then came reorganisation beyond January, B and C Squadrons halt to gather strength and reinforcements, they declared they had only enough men left to attempt one more gap as the others had been so expensive in men and materials. At this juncture we passed through gap two, tanks and anti-tank guns are already there with the Rifle Brigade and assault troops firing loosely with bren-guns. Fire was being returned by tracers which often ricocheted off the armour. Artillery intenser, if possible, and more concentrated on the ridge, we often had to duck shrapnel and blast. Scorpion [tank] was reported out of action in gap two and a mechanical defect was quickly repaired. One in gap four received a direct hit and was out of action immediately, none left to carry on to February. Major Wittington had gout and was not able to move easily. He sat in his jeep with binoculars on the horizon watching the gun flashes and calmly advising the digging troops when to duck as the shells came over.[3]

As the minefield task force advanced behind the 1/7th Queens they were impeded by soft sand and damaging enemy fire from the start, they had to fight their way through before they could start the gaps through the minefields that they were required to

3 Manuscript sent to author by R.J. Jeffery 1989.

make. The flailing Scorpions crawled forward in great clouds of sand and dust amid the roar of their engines. Those that did not break down or hit mines were soon picked off by enemy anti-tank fire and the engineers were then forced to lift the mines by hand, prodding the ground with their 18 inch bayonets. They worked steadily with the noise of battle roaring around them and shells and bullets wining over their heads.

Trooper J. Ruane, Royal Tank Regiment, watched the sappers in awe:

> The sight of sappers lining up and going forward to probe for mines with bayonets was terrible and awe inspiring to watch. Every one of them deserved a medal, as they seemed to go to certain death. They no sooner went over than bursts of enemy machine-gun fire seemed to wipe them out. Then another line would form up, stub their cigarettes out and move over the top. It was a privilege to be in the company of such men.[4]

Sappers prodding the ground with their eighteen inch bayonets as they search for mines while under fire. (Author's collection)

Trooper J.W. Telford, 1st Battalion Royal Tank Regiment, recalls the almost surreal scene that met his eyes and assailed his senses:

> Tremendous artillery barrage, strange sort of echoing as if we were under an immense dome. Continuous gun flashes made a most weird sort of nightmarish light. We set off excited and breathless with that orchestral music of the continuous gun-fire in the background. I remember seeing a young captain

4 Interview with author. J. Ruane 1991.

> walking behind a Scorpion [tank] intent on supervising the job. Something seemed to worry him, and he literally screamed at the crew and someone nearby. On edge poor devil, some job. Our chaps on the ground looked a bit grim and drawn. I suppose it was all that sand that made it a sort of ghoulish nightmarish day by the seaside, enlivened by Lt Adams tank burning.[5]

British tanks of the 7th Armoured Division move off in line formation. (Author's collection)

Lt Leslie R. Symonds, 44th Reconnaissance Regiment, advanced on foot with his men into a storm of fire through the minefield gap:

> The men crouch as they walk, I walk, I mustn't show fear as they are watching me. The Engineers are superb, ignoring the shells they move forward sounding for mines with bayonets, screwing in iron pickets to mark the edges of the cleared areas and attaching white tapes to mark the path and my God they are even fitting battery lamps, shaded from the enemy but lighting the way for our own troops. We move with them, 10, 50, 100 yards, a shell bursts seemingly on top of us and we fall flat. Stones and splinters rattle around seemingly for many seconds after the burst. A corporal limps towards me, I shudder, one side

5 Letter to author J.W. Telford 1994.

of his face is raw and one of his thighs. His left arm is hanging loose. Carrying out orders we lay him on the ground and give him some water, sticking his rifle in the ground with his helmet on top. The medical lads will be following up behind us, the men are looking sick and I expect I am too, this is our first casualty. I force myself to smile as we go forward again. We climb a ridge and start down the other side, there is a metallic crash ahead, the anti-mine tank [Scorpion] has been hit. A very light soars up, red, white, green, those are the recognition colours painted on our baggage when we left England. As this stupid thought comes to my mind machine-guns suddenly open up on us, not only from the front, but from left and right as well. Streams of red and white tracer bullets pour into the midst of us. We must move forward yard by yard now and at a crouch. Another murderous burst of fire from the front and then from each side as well, by this time we have moved into a slight hollow and the pattern of enfilade tracers are criss-crossing above our heads. I must have something heavier; I look around and see the trooper the others call Goofy, big as a horse and nervous as a kitten. I write rapidly on a message form then watch Goofy scramble safely back over the ridge with a message asking for mortar support.[6]

Troops advancing into clouds of dust and smoke on the battlefield. (Author's collection)

6 Manuscript sent to author by L.R. Symonds 1991.

It was not until 02:30 a.m. on the 24th that gaps had been cleared through the January minefield and only then when the Rifle Brigade had taken out several enemy posts that were being particularly troublesome. Carriers of the Reconnaissance Regiment tried to pass through the gaps and were hit by anti-tank fire, leaving them black and burning in the lanes. By 04:00 a.m. the 5th Battalion Royal Tank Regiment, the Scots Greys and two companies of the Rifle Brigade had got through.

Pte Douglas Waller, Anti-Tank gunner, 1st Rifle Brigade, recalls the tough opposition they faced from the Italian Folgore Parachute Division:

> We started the battle in the south opposite the Italian Folgore Division, which contrary to the general opinion of Italian troops were really tough nuts. We went in and got through the first minefield and were in the gap when our portee [truck] got hit in the engine, probably a solid shot because there wasn't a big explosion. We just heard a clang as something hit the front of the truck and it folded up. We were then useless because we couldn't drag the anti-tank gun through the soft sand, and we joined an infantry company and spent the first night attacking strong points. It was very hairy because they were well dug in, some came out to surrender and others would go on firing. We suffered quite a few casualties. Bill Ash was with me and we came under heavy mortar fire, we went in at platoon strength and suddenly Bill and I were the only ones left standing, all the others were either killed or wounded. Mortar fire is very frightening as you can't hear the bombs coming. The fighting went on all night, the tops of the enemy pits were covered with sandbags, corrugated tin or wood. You had to clear these, the machine-gun nests and mortar pits were the most difficult to winkle out. You ran in short bursts, covered by others as you did so and if the pit was open you could toss in a grenade.[7]

From a range of 2,000 yards an Italian gun was firing on one of the gaps with great effect and the casualties started to mount, the flash from its muzzle could be seen stabbing the night. Lt Colonel Freddie Stephens, C/O 1st Rifle Brigade, studied the enemy position in the moonlight and ordered up a machine-gun platoon, the guns were mounted on trucks and were soon brought into action killing all the Italian gun crew.

Rifleman Harry Suckling of the Rifle Brigade helped guard one of the minefield gaps:

> We were protecting the gap in the minefield and had good slit trenches because of the shelling, Gerry started to shell us, and the last shell landed close by. A

7 Ibid., D. Waller 1995.

Stretcher bearers bring in a wounded man. (Author's collection)

> lump of shrapnel went past me, didn't touch my arm but seared it and hit a corporal in the thigh. When you get a lump of shrapnel hitting you it makes a bigger hole coming out than going in, like a bullet does, he had a terrific wound. I thought he'd lose his leg, but we got a couple of field dressings and patched him up. He came back a few months later. One lad I knew was wounded three times and came back each time, I asked him why he came back and he said he missed the lads, the fourth time he was killed.[8]

Rifleman Fred Cooper served in a mortar section and was attached to the Rifle Brigade:

> Being in battle was like being drugged or drunk, we were so tired and didn't know what was happening. When we looked back the sky was clear to the east and looking to the west was like looking at a wall of sand, churned up by artillery fire and tanks. We had a tough day and my mortar section of seven blokes had four casualties in 15 minutes. We attacked with the tanks and tried to make a wedge and drive it in, but because we were in a wedge the enemy could fire on us from both sides and from the front. We got such a concentration of fire

8 J. Sadler, *El Alamein* (Stroud: Amberley Publishing, 2012), p. 159.

> we had to pull back. On top of a ridge were six burning Sherman tanks, one was white hot, glowing like a light bulb, the others were various shades of red.[9]

British mortar team in action. (Author's collection)

Lt H.L. Mathews was with the 1/7th Queens:

> I remember shells and mortar fire coming from the enemy, we advanced through bursts and through the smoke and dust. A runner came up to me and shouted in my ear 'Mr Davies is wounded take over', Mr Davies was my platoon commander. Suddenly I realised that our numbers were getting fewer. Then we were called by Colonel Burton and Major Colbrook, my company commander, the Colonel called us to him shouting 'we are in our own barrage, back 100 paces'. We re-grouped but there was only 12 of us left and we decided to turn south and link up with the Free French who were advancing on our left but they had not got to their objective. We stumbled into the rear of an Italian strongpoint that turned out to be manned by part of a battalion of the Folgore Parachute Division and we were captured. We spent the night under guard in comparative quietness. In the morning they tried to march us away but we decided to make a break for it. As we did so we were fired on by our own tanks,

9 Interview with author. F. Cooper 1991.

which appeared like little black lumps on the skyline about a mile away. In the confusion we ran a few yards then fell flat, we were nearly half way back when it got light and our tanks started firing at us again, we just had to lay there not daring to move but holding a couple of British helmets towards our tanks hoping they would see we were British. I think it was an hour or so before they stopped firing at us and then a carrier and a Honey Tank started to move out towards us. By now the Colonel, who was next to me, had been killed. Major Colbrook was fatally wounded and had been left with the Italians who had a doctor. Major Mills, who was near me shouted 'when I say go, go' and again we made a mad dash a few yards at a time. I made for the carrier, reached it and jumped inside. It was commanded by a corporal of the Rifle Brigade, I remember him standing in the carrier while we were cowering in the bottom of it. He stood there as we turned for our own lines with tracer whizzing past, even anti-tank tracer, he gave the Ities a rude sign with his fingers. I heard him shout 'they couldn't hit fuck all'. He took us back through the tanks and infantry to relative peace and quiet behind the ridge.[10]

Eighth Army soldier manning his Vickers heavy machine-gun in a slit trench. (Author's collection)

10 Manuscript sent to author by H.L. Mathews 1995.

Lt Leslie R. Symonds, 44th Reconnaissance Regiment, was pinned down with his men by heavy machine-gun fire and waited for the arrival of mortar teams:

> I put the lads in fire positions while we waited, they are lying flat. I am kneeling and kidding myself I am being brave. Someone is walking towards us from the front and a shout goes up: 'don't shoot it's Mr Day'. Mike Day, along with three other subalterns on the other gaps, has had the worst job of all tonight. The anti-mine device on the tanks [Scorpions] obstructs the drivers view and Mike's job has been to sit up by the turret as a guide. The tank must have been hit as Mike is walking towards us oblivious of the machine-gun fire, as though he is on an afternoon stroll. He must get hit, the bloody fool, the brave bloody idiot. He drops down by my side now and says, 'hello Les, the tank's been hit, knocked out'. Mike's sentence ends in a scream as he falls beside me holding his stomach with both hands, I lay him flat out in a comfortable position, but he does not seem in pain now. After a minute or so he speaks: 'this is mine Les'. Don't be a fool Mike you'll soon be back with the medicos, 'afraid not Les, the bastards have got me through the guts, no chance. There is a letter to my mother in my pocket, will you see she gets it'. I find the letter in his breast pocket and it is already soaked in blood. 'OK Mike I have it'. He is silent while the battle continues around us then he says, 'are you there Les?' I hold his hand and he says melodramatically 'the gap must go through you know, good luck Les, Goodbye' and Mike Day is dead. Suddenly I realise that two carriers fitted with mortars are over the ridge and coming to join us, Alan Tew jumps out of the first carrier and as he does so gets a bullet through the leg and as he falls gets a bullet through the other leg, shouting out 'oh the bastards'. Sergeant Bingham is with the other mortar and he needs no instruction. Within seconds three inch mortar bombs are being hurled at one of the machine-gun posts which falls silent. First class, now try the other one. My order is drowned out by two sharp crashes. Within a few seconds both carriers have been hit, Christ! They must have their anti-tank guns with their forward infantry. They could only get that accuracy by open sight shooting; it means too that they can see the carriers and know exactly where we are. That sinks us, not too pleasant certainly, I ask my sergeant how many men left? 'eight sir'. I must do something and stand to my feet; a splatter of bullets drops amongst us. Then there is a sudden flash and a bang so near that there is no warning swish. Their mortars have pinpointed us and if we move their machine-guns get us, if we stay their mortars will. I again stand to my feet grasping my tommy gun, there is a crash, the world is coming to pieces around me, the tommy gun flies through the air and I am hurled to the ground. I hear a voice filled with despair calling out, 'they have got Mr Symonds'. What is wrong with my arm? I look down at my middle where it feels to be, it is not there, it is lying above my head, oh God it

> is knocked off. No, it is still joined and only as I lift it down and lay it across my chest do I feel the agony of it. I raise my head and look around, no longer is anyone in fire positions, a few are groaning. I need not think now, I am so tired, so tired, I pray a little. I think a little of you my darling Peg. There seems to be no small arms fire now, but the mortar bombs are falling still, but only occasionally.[11]

The 2nd Free French Brigade, on the extreme left flank, launched an assault by two of its battalions on 24th October attacking over the rugged terrain of Mount Himeimat, they also faced massive difficulties. As the French flying column launched an infantry assault on the twin peaks of Mount Himeimat, they would be confronted with strong opposition in the form of the Italian Folgore Parachute Division who held all the high ground. This attack was an essential component of the Eighth Army's overall operations in the south and by taking this hill would take possession of the key observation post that overlooked the entire British line in the southern sector. If the British held this position they would have a distinct advantage by being able to direct their own artillery fire onto the enemies' right flank and then outflank the Axis Forces southern defences. The first French objective was to be the smaller feature of the Naqb Rala Plateau, followed by the eliminating of the Italian positions on Mount Himeimat. If this was successfully completed they could then link up with 7th Armoured Division who would then press on to the rear of the axis positions.

Prior to this operation XIII Corps commander, General Horrocks, and the French commander, General Marie Pierre Koenig, had been involved in heated discussions regarding the feasibility of the operation. Koenig argued that he did not have enough tanks and heavy artillery to soften up the enemy positions and that the long approach march meant his men would be exposed to axis artillery and air attacks. Horrocks insisted and told the French commander that if his brigade would not do it he would get one that would, reluctantly Koenig conceded.

At 19:30 p.m. on 23rd October the two French Foreign Legion Battalions approached the southern flank of Naqb Rala. At 20:30 p.m. a creeping barrage crashed down upon the Italian positions and lasted for nearly two hours. Baltimore bombers roared overhead dropping their bombs and adding to the confusion and disruption. To stop the French infantry advance the paratroopers put down a hail of machine-gun and mortar fire on the Frenchmen as they approached the Italian outer defences, taking heavy casualties in the process. Undeterred the French pressed home their attack uphill and overran machine-gun posts on the outer perimeter killing or capturing the crews. The Frenchmen then moved into the main Italian positions and came under a heavy barrage of mortar fire which caused many more casualties.

11 Manuscript sent to author by L.R. Symonds 1991.

Men of 2nd Free French Brigade receive their battle honours. (Author's collection)

The Italian paratroopers allowed the Frenchmen to move well into their main positions until they found themselves caught on an open plateau, here the paratroopers counter-attacked vigorously, they hurled grenades and shot up the French units forcing them to retreat through the mortar fire that fell all around them causing even more casualties and adding to their misery. The sand in the attack area was so soft that it prevented the French from dragging their anti-tank guns forward to keep up with the main thrust. The French were caught off guard by unexpected counter-attacks coming from three different directions and the paratroopers, though under heavy machine-gun fire, continued the pursuit of their foes downhill preventing them from rallying, the chase then turned into a rout. Foreign Legion troops were then counter-attacked by the tanks and infantry of the German Keil Group and were slowly forced to give ground under the unrelenting assault by the Germans and Italians. One great blow to French moral on the morning of 24th October was the death of one of their most flamboyant officers, the Russian Prince Colonel Dimitri Amilakvari who was caught in the enemy shell-fire and hit. As the French pulled back the German armoured and artillery units rained down a terrible fire on the them, soft skinned vehicles went up in flames and the paratroopers of the Folgore added to the disruption with their own artillery, mortar and machine-gun fire. Many of the French troops' weapons had to be abandoned on the battle-field. Early on 24th the defending axis troops looked out over a landscape strewn with the dead of both sides and their abandoned weapons. The scantily held Italian positions now regrouped as the Desert Air Force commenced numerous bombing raids on the Himeimat area. While this was happening the German artillery spotters on Mount Himeimat played havoc with the advancing troops of the 44th Division on the right and the tanks of the 7th Armoured Division.

Colonel Dimitri Amilakvari, French Foreign Legion. Killed in action 24th October 1942. (Author's collection)

Shortly after 05:00 a.m. on 24th November the minefield task force on 44th Division's front set out to clear gaps through the February minefield, but as its numbers were greatly reduced it could only start two gaps and did not have the man power to attempt four. As daylight dawned on 24th enemy artillery and anti-tank gun fire increased hampering the sappers as they laboured to lift mines by hand.

Sapper John Harris, Royal Engineers, knew that the enemy had laid a number of different types of mines and that it was the job of him and his comrades to clear them for the tanks and infantry to pass through:

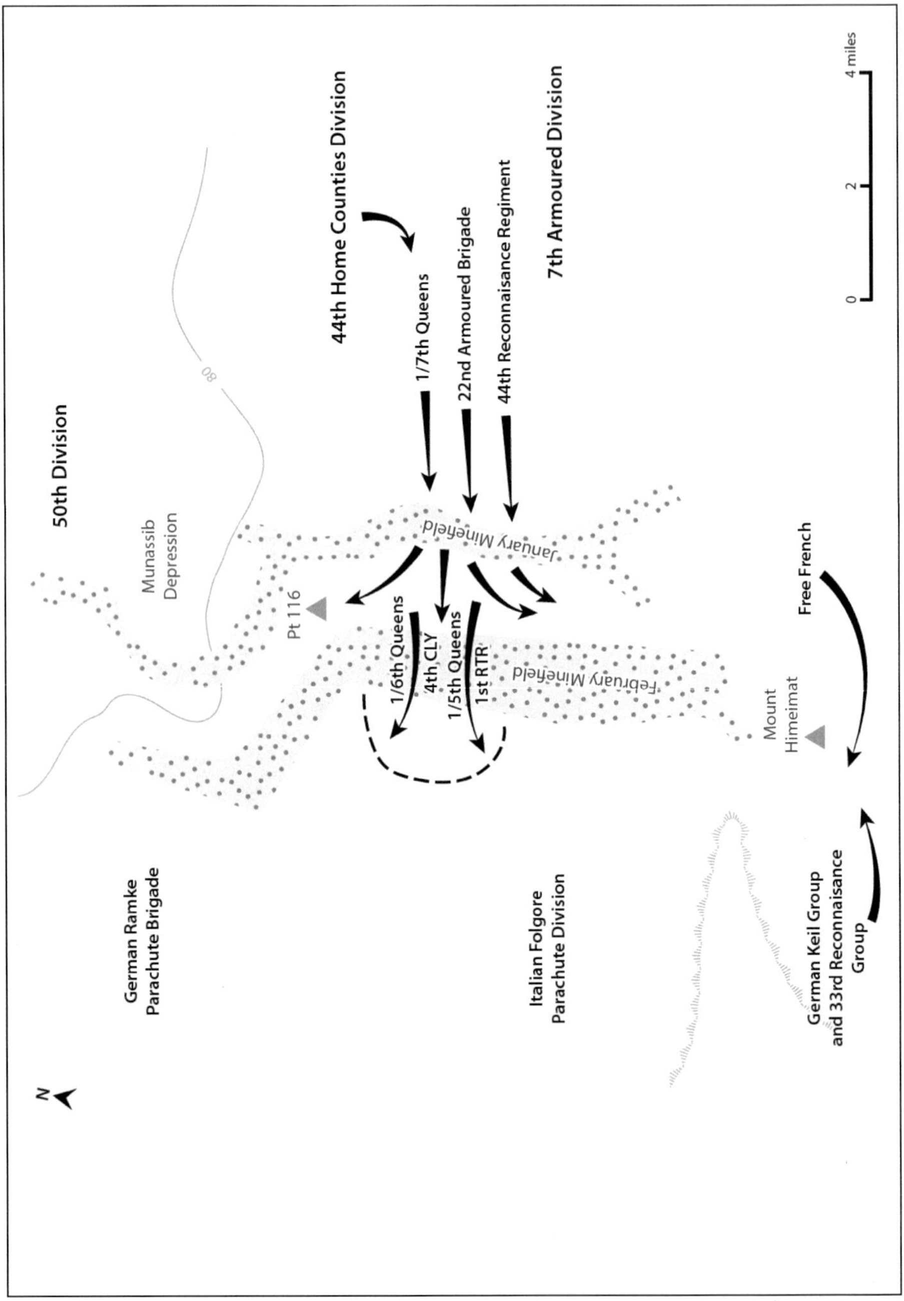

The 44th Home Counties Division and 7th Armoured Division 23rd to 26th October 1942.

> One of the most nerve wracking things in mine clearing was finding out where the front edge of a field was located. It was really a hit or miss affair and to confuse us Gerry often mixed in the normal anti-tank minefields with anti-personnel mines. We were told about a new mine called S Mines, which were buried up to the depth of a three pronged detonator. The whole thing looked like a tin of baked beans with a nozzle on top, but of course all that was visible were the three prongs of the detonator. When a foot trod on the detonator there were two distinct explosions, the first flung the mine up into the air and the second explosion was at waist height and it spewed out hundreds of ball bearings horizontally at great speed. You can guess the effect of those things and how we felt about them. There were other types of anti-personnel mines as well. Behind each sweeper was a three man lifting party, who knelt down and felt around each mine to make sure that it was a clean one, that is that it didn't have trip wires running from it or booby traps attached to it. That really was a dodgy operation because Gerry also had an explosive device that might be fitted under the fuse in the body of the mine. Anyway once a mine had been defused it was lifted out of the ground and placed outside the marking tape, the gap markers ran out their white tapes to keep pace with the lifters and so follow up troops could see their path marked clearly on both sides. The length of time taken was increased if we were under heavy shell fire, longer still if we were under Spandau fire and even longer if we had casualties. Everybody moved dead slow then, relying on the prodding with the bayonet method. We worked in half hour shifts, any longer than that and we lost concentration and became careless.[12]

The 22nd Armoured Brigade had held the gaps made in the January minefield at a cost of over 200 casualties. Brigadier Roberts went forward to see what exactly was going on and found a scene of utter chaos. Facing in all directions were the burning and blackened tank hulks, vehicles and carriers with enemy shells falling all around.

Cpl Peter Roach, 1st Royal Tank Regiment, described the approach march to their start line:

> We moved off in the dark, a winding snake of vehicles each wrapped in its own cloud of dust, each towing empty petrol cans to accentuate the noise, dust and the size of the approaching threat. I listened to the voices on the radio and recognised the boredom, the fear, the exasperation and the excitement. This was my world, hot in the extreme, full of fine blowing dust, noisy, cramped and blind. Should we fight my job was loading the Sherman guns. It grew dark

12 Interview with author. J. Harris 1993.

> and we moved again to the external chaos of an advance. The leading tanks ran into trouble in the minefield gaps. The Colonel was desperately trying to elicit the facts from scared and harried tank commanders, who in turn were trying to elicit the facts from scared engineers who were clearing the minefields, who were trying to elicit the facts from the crew of a tank immobilised and shocked by the explosion of a mine.[13]

All day on the 24th October continuous artillery and mortar fire plagued the 44th Home Counties Division and 7th Armoured Division in their narrow and congested bridgehead, doggedly the infantry held on to the bare ground they had won between January and February minefields. The enemy armour held off at a distance in hull down positions watching events unfold. In the heat of the day with the sun high in the sky the desert shimmered and the salient continued to be swept by enemy fire making any reconnaissance impossible and the locating of any enemy posts with any accuracy hard to do.

An enemy barrage comes down on the carriers and vehicles of the minefield task force. (Author's collection)

In the northern coastal sector on 24th an important event occurred, early that morning General Stumme, commander of the Afrika Korps, needed to learn first-hand the state of affairs and went to the front to see for himself the area being attacked by

13 Letter sent to author by P. Roach 1994.

9th Australian Division. An officer that was accompanying him was shot dead at his side and Stumme died of a heart attack, Lt General Ritter von Thoma then assumed command of the Axis Forces. Rommel returned on the night of the 25th and assumed command once again, though he was far from fit to do so.

On the night of the 24th in the south the attack on the February minefield was resumed by the 1/5th and 1/6th Battalions of the Queen's Regiment. They formed up just beyond the foremost tanks and advanced under a barrage. Keeping close to the barrage they advanced 2,500 yards and thrust right through the February minefield, consolidating a defensive position half a mile beyond it.

Pte S. Gray, 1/6th Queens, recalls the action as his unit pressed on through February minefield:

> We moved up to where the tanks were waiting for the off. The time came for us to fix bayonets and get to the tapes then we moved off. The creeping barrage started and in no time at all there was screaming and crying out in pain as the men were stepping on anti-personnel mines. Our artillery was screaming over our heads and after a while, though you could not say you got used to it, our minds just blocked out all the noise and we carried on as if we were on a stunt back home. [14]

Pte T.V. Pulland was with the 1/5th Queens as they left their start line, as they moved on anti-personnel mines took a steady toll:

> Even before we left the start line we were under fire from Gerry artillery. The battalion had moved in single file down through the Twyford Gap in our Nuts minefield, the track was lit by little amber lights on poles. Our barrage had been firing for a long time, but we were soon aware that the enemy was firing back. It was not possible to see the shell bursts unless you were very near them, the dust that they flung up hid the flashes of the explosions, but men were falling all over the place hit by shrapnel. Then the further we got into the minefield the more fierce was the fire. And it wasn't only shells, but mortars and machine-guns firing tracer. Behind us was the gapping detachment but by the time we had crossed no man's land we were very tired. The going was terrible, it was mostly very soft sand and hard to walk through. Then we were in the February minefield, at least we were told that we had entered it. There was no difference as far as I could see between no man's land and the Gerry minefield, but once we knew for sure that we were in unswept areas we all had a horrible feeling,

14 *Battle of El Alamein: Queen's Royal West Surrey Regiment* <www.queensroyalsurreys.org.uk/ww2/middle_east>.

> I can't describe it but you have the fear that the next step you take is going to be your last. Of course most of the mines were anti-tank but we all knew that among them Gerry would sow some anti-personnel ones as well. There were lots of red devils about, you know those Italian hand grenades, and there were lots of empty slit trenches around us. The battle-field was completely empty so far as I can recall, and I can't remember seeing any enemy dead or alive. There were so many explosions and of course I was concentrating so hard on looking out for S mines that nothing else seemed to matter.[15]

Pte S. Gray, 1/6th Queens, moved with his unit into the enemy positions:

> Passing through the minefield I had a chap at the side of me with a tommy gun. The first trench load of the enemy we came across the chap with the tommy gun just opened fire on them, they had no fight left in them and were lying on top of one another. I left him and went forward and came across another trench full, they were in long trenches which held 20 odd soldiers. They were kneeling and leaning on one another and I would have got no pleasure from shooting them in the back, so I shouted and swore at them to get out. We were not allowed to take POWs back nor were we allowed to take our own wounded back. What I wanted to do if I got them all out would be to point in the direction I wanted them to go. Unfortunately for them in front of us behind the dannert wire the Germans were on the high ground and could see at least our shadows if not us. Then a shell came over and landed right on them, it blew them to pieces, but I felt nothing. I then moved forward and came under heavy machine-gun fire, I hit the deck and my officer [Lt ACF Norman] was at the side of me. Every time I tried to move there was more fire, in fact it was impossible to move without being shot to pieces.[16]

There they awaited the arrival of the British tanks; their hastily made position was very exposed and was under constant heavy fire from the long open flanks. To their rear the sappers worked under a storm of flying steel and succeeded in clearing two lanes through mines thickly laid, done mostly by hand with bayonet prodding. This great feat of arms had been conducted with courage and determination and had cost the Sappers dearly in casualties.

15 Manuscript sent to author by T V Pulland. 1992.

16 *Queen's Royal West Surrey Regiment* <www.queensroyalsurreys.org.uk/ww2/middle_east> (Accessed November 2018).

Troops take cover as they watch out for the ever present enemy, Mount Himeimat in the distance. (Courtesy of Wilfred Gilson)

Sapper F Hesslewood, Royal Engineers, was on a night reconnaissance patrol with an officer, Captain Smith of the 1/5th Queen's Regiment, searching for gaps in the minefields:

> I had to search the ground in front of the wire and a favourite trick of Gerry was to plant a few anti-personnel mines in front of the wire to deter people like me. I found nothing and my three companions joined me at the point of the wire where I intended to enter the minefield. As we stood at the wire we were surprised to hear a voice singing a very lovely song. The singer had a good voice and we paused momentarily to listen as the Italian words floated over the desert. The singer probably wouldn't have been in the mood for love songs had he known that four British Tommies were nearby. As I worked I had no idea of the width of the minefield, the wire on the other side was not visible, but I knew from the singer that there must be troops guarding the inside wire. My comrades covered me and held open the wires whilst I used my bayonet inside the fence to feel the ground and obtain enough clear ground to get myself in a working position. It's hard work sounding for mines on hands and knees and progress was slow. My heart was beating so loudly that I was sure they must hear it and if they looked towards me I felt sure that I could not escape being seen in the bright moonlight. I looked back from whence I had come and could see no wire and no patrol. Without doubt I had never been so alone in my life.

> I realised I must go on, I glanced up and to my great consternation and horror I saw at about 30 yards range a person in the lying/load position about to shoot me. I fell flat on my face instinctively and remained in that position without moving a muscle for what seemed like hours but was probably a few minutes. All the time I kept thinking why doesn't he shoot? why no call for surrender? I decided to risk a squint in the direction of my adversary and saw him in exactly the same position as before. It was then I decided that if it wasn't dead I had better do something as I couldn't lie in this position forever. I decided I should have a closer look as I had nothing to lose, I continued sounding and crawling until I came up to my assailant, who turned out to be three petrol tins in such a position so as to resemble a man in the moonlight. I was rather annoyed that they were British tins and I blamed them for nearly bringing to an end a not very promising career.[17]

The C/O of the 1/5th Queens, Lt Colonel Lance East, led the battalion forward across the 1,000 yard wide February minefield:

> We suffered casualties from booby traps attached to the barbed wire. Private Leonard Mansell was blown to pieces by one of them. Ted Sarginson's platoon on my right had a number of casualties owing to one gun [from our own supporting barrage] firing short. Major Cooper leading the way on a compass bearing outdistanced everyone until he was hit by machine-gun fire. We had reached our objective having cleared the minefield and were in close contact with the enemy. There was a period of confusion in the darkness while we vainly attempted to regroup and advance further. We occupied our slit trench/sangar for the next 17 hours and the battalion suffered heavy casualties from mortar fire.[18]

Pte T.V. Pulland:

> The enemy seemed to be trying to cut our companies off from each other and in that way to isolate them. The Gerries and Ities were firing tracer from their machine-guns, a lot of it was fixed line firing so that it was quite possible to walk alongside the tracer line, not too close of course. It was clear to us later on that by avoiding the tracer bullets we were being forced into ground that Gerry was saturating with mortar fire, we were being controlled and herded to where he would be able to kill us. We seemed to have been marching for hours

17 Interview with author. F. Hesslewood 1991.
18 P. Delaforce, *Churchill's Desert Rats* (Stroud: Sutton Publishing, 2002]), p 121.

and then there was a certain amount of confusion and we began to dig in. It seemed we had passed through January minefield and that we had reached our objective 800 yards on the far side of February minefield, here we were pinned down and it was very uncomfortable for everybody concerned. I was lying down in an Itie slit trench that had been used as a latrine, my mates never came near me for days afterwards. One of our casualties was a man who took cover under a two pounder anti-tank gun, Gerry fire went through both tyres and the full weight of the gun went down on his back. The regimental history tells us that the forward troops were counter attacked by the Italian Folgore Division and taken prisoner, the rest of us were pulled back to guard the gap that had just been pushed through the minefield [February], after a couple of hours we were ordered forward again, it was all very confusing.[19]

Captured German anti-tank guns. (Author's collection)

Lt D.J. Watson, 1/5th Queen's Regiment:

We set off across 1,000 yards of minefield led by an officer on a compass bearing and Lt Colonel East using a stick as a result of a First World War wound. We were to advance behind a barrage and there were casualties in the platoon on my

19 Manuscript sent to author by T.V. Pulland 1992.

> right because of a gun [ours] firing short. I can still remember the shriek from one of my platoon when a booby trap on the wire exploded and literally blew him to pieces. Eventually our leading platoon and the 1/6th Queens arrived in the middle of the Italian positions and some 20 or 30 Italians cheerfully gave themselves up. The remainder of the Folgore Division however were made of sterner stuff and proceeded to inflict heavy casualties on us, using mortars and machine-guns firing from entrenched positions. I remember young O'Connell, both legs severed by a mortar bomb, screaming for help and then for his mother before he mercifully died. Major Capper, who led the advance, was hit and disappeared from sight, but called out deliriously at intervals during the day before he too fell silent. When the barrage stopped the advance stopped, we had reached our objective and were in close contact with the enemy. After a period of confusion in the darkness while we vainly attempted to regroup and advance further, I found myself sharing a slit trench with Sergeant Parkin, we occupied that slit trench for the next 12 hours. When daylight came it was dangerous to lift your head and suicide to stand up. We had bully, biscuits and the water from our bottles. An officer, Lt Opperman, was sent back before first light to ask for tanks to come forward in support, he was awarded the MC for this hazardous task. As dusk approached those forward of us who were in a position to observe the enemy reported they were gathering in force for an attack. The plans for a rearguard action were overtaken by a sudden rush of Italians, so we got up and ran. I can still chuckle at the thought that not only did our prisoners run with us but a few of the attackers joined us as well. I could not recall crossing the 1,000 yards of February minefield again or two considerable wire fences but I can still see the welcome line of our tanks who started up and opened fire as we approached. I think I was more frightened after the battle than before or during. In the advance I was keyed up to meet the physical demands made on me, but once in the slit trench the dynamism of the advance having been lost, I had rather a dumb acceptance, like a cow in a slaughter house.[20]

Here things went badly awry, the infantry and sappers had advanced on different axes and lost touch with each other. As the paratroopers of the Folgore Division, with the support of German heavy artillery, smashed into the British assault confusion piled upon confusion. Individual explosions could no longer be distinguished as they blended into one continuous roar.

When the tanks of the City of London Yeomanry and 1st Battalion Royal Tank Regiment moved up through the newly opened lanes they found themselves under

20 Manuscript sent to author by W. Harrison 1996.

heavy anti-tank fire from guns the infantry in their haste had missed. It was not long before the exits from the February minefield were completely blocked with burning tanks, others that tried to get round them were blown up by scattered mines. 31 knocked out and burning tanks and vehicles now blocked the exits and further headway was impossible without losing more precious tanks.

Stuka dive-bombers flew in squadrons; they would dive vertically out of the sky one after the other accompanied by a loud and terrifying howl before unloading bombs on the unlucky recipients. (Author's collection)

The County of London Yeomanry lost a total of 26 tanks as it tried to pass through the gap in February minefield, Harry Ramsbottom, Middlesex Yeomanry Signals, was attached to 4th County of London Yeomanry for the attack:

> The anti-tank defences opened fire on fixed lines, within seconds it seemed as though the whole war was revolving around the regiment with bursting shells and tracer illuminating the scene. There were many nasty moments. It was difficult to tell when the tank was clear of the minefield in this inferno. It was a helpless position with gunners trying to machine-gun the unseen foe, but being unable to bring accurate fire to bear. Lt P M R Scott the CO had his tank knocked out, Major David Silvertop the 2 i/c did wonders, Lt Neville Gillman

was wounded and lost a leg, 2nd Lt Neville Thomas Burrell and Trooper Ronald Stanley Torlot killed, Tony Torlot captured.[21]

German 88 crew preparing for action. (Courtesy of H. Wernamann)

Lt R.J. Jeffery, 44th Reconnaissance Regiment, moved in his carrier towards February minefield:

> We moved towards the minefield up to 700 yards but found nothing, it was suspected it was further on. We wandered around in the carrier through the hellish barrage, often ducking and smoking as we liked. We had been given a tot of rum by the Adjutant who was himself comfortably plastered. After this relaxer we felt better. Until at one unfortunate juncture one burst of shrapnel bounced off the hard rock, missed Jock and burst into the carrier where I was operating the set. I was hit in the face and knee. The Adjutant guided me to a slit trench and I was told to walk through the minefield to an RAP [Regimental

21 Letter to author H. Ramsbottom 1991.

> Aid Post] which was in a hollow. It was a nightmare walk, the shelling was terrific and the small arms fire was whistling everywhere and tracer bullets were weaving a pattern in the sky. One Scorpion tank was stranded in the middle of number four gap with chaps using it for cover. Half way down the track I met Sergeant Hitchens who thankfully escorted me back to the RAP.[22]

Colonel East, 1/6th Queens, was hit and left unconscious to be picked up the next morning:

> I had been shot through the leg, shrapnel went into my left thigh and I was picked up next morning and taken to enemy trenches in the rear which we had passed earlier. When I stood up I noticed a mortar bomb stuck in the rock an inch or two from my head. It had not gone off and in retrospect I realised I had been temporarily unconscious when it had landed.[23]

The attempt to breach the February minefield had failed. The infantry of the 44th Home Counties Division had been targeted by heavy enemy fire and remained in their make-shift trenches in the shallow bridge head, pinned to the ground by a resolute enemy that showed no signs of withdrawal.

Brigadier Roberts, C/O 22nd Armoured Brigade, saw the trouble his tanks were having trying to force a path through the minefields:

> Our main effort to make gaps in the minefields was to be done by these Scorpions which were very unreliable, and the Scorpions broke down and got in the away, the Sappers had to come up and do it by hand, there was a great deal of delay. And after the first night all we'd got through was the first minefield, we then sat between the minefields and Himeimat was there within 2,000 yards, absolutely looking down on us. It was a most uncomfortable situation. We tried again the next night and then we didn't have the Scorpions working, we only had the Sappers and the Queens Regiment. Somehow or other, I couldn't tell you how, the Queens Regiment went one way and the Sappers another and we went where the gap was and there was no infantry there. Then we got every tank knocked out by mines or anti-tank fire, we struggled all night and made no progress, we came back.[24]

22 Manuscript sent to author by R.J. Jeffery 1989.
23 *Queen's Royal West Surrey Regiment* <www.queensroyalsurreys.org.uk/ww2/middle_east>
24 R. Kershaw, *Tank Men* (London: Hodder and Stoughton, 2008), p. 231.

Italian sappers laying anti-tank mines. (Author's collection)

General John Harding commanding the 7th Armoured Division recalled his tank units to prevent any further losses:

> The minefields in the north caused most trouble, if you are stuck in a minefield you are a dead duck to anti-tank fire. The first night the French got a foothold on Himeimat but were driven back. We did get through the minefields but started to lose tanks and because I had the restriction on me not to lose too many I decided to halt the attack and hold what we had. We were stuck.[25]

The infantry of the 1/5th and 1/6th Queen's held on tenaciously to their exposed bridgehead, enemy posts, some as close as 100 yards, fired on them and the wounded were in deep distress as they could not be evacuated to the rear. The whole area for miles around was under direct enemy observation from Mount Himeimat and the observers could call down artillery fire whenever they saw movement, for the men in the bridgehead it was a terrifying experience. On the evening of the 25th the armour was withdrawn leaving the infantry totally isolated.

2nd Lt P.B. Kingsford, 1/5th Queens, came under heavy fire on the 25th:

25 C.E. Lucas-Philips, *Alamein* (London: Heinemann, 1962) p. 84.

> The 1/6th Queens were on our left, but they were being very heavily shelled and mortared during the 25th. No tanks got through to support us as the gap in the minefield was being enfiladed from el Himeimat [two pimples] which had been recaptured by the Germans recently.[26]

Pte S. Gray, 1/6th Queens, and his comrades that had survived got the order to pull back:

> So after quite a long while lying in the open and not daring to move it was on the point of getting light. I said to the officer [Lt A C F Norman] 'it's coming to sun up then they will pick us off'. He said, 'Pass the word around, it's every man for himself and find a hole to get into.' Strange as it seemed a cloud came over the moon which gave us the chance to move. But as we did so over came mortars and shells which got some of the chaps, I and another chap found an empty German trench. Mortar and shell-fire kept coming in our direction but eventually we got back to our own lines. Only three of us who had been at the dannert wire got back, they were Lt Norman, Alf Doyle, who came from Holborn in London and myself.[27]

The reality of war: A knocked-out German tank with a dead crewman next to his once powerful machine. (Author's collection)

26 *Queen's Royal West Surrey Regiment* <www.queensroyalsurreys.org.uk/ww2/middle_east>
27 Ibid.

The troops of the Queen's Regiment, having stuck to their guns with dogged determination amid the storm of battle, were withdrawn that night to a position between January and February minefields, during the retreat more casualties were taken as the enemy kept up an intense artillery fire in the area. A great feat of arms had been performed here by the infantry, a feat that has received little mention in any major history of the Battle of Alamein.

In the extreme south near Naqb Rala, the Free French's objective, cannon firing Hurricanes attacked the tanks of the Keil Group who were armed with captured British Stuart tanks [Honeys], Hurricanes destroyed seven of them and put out of action another five. On the afternoon of 24th the main activity along the front was in the air. In the course of the day the desert air force flew 1,500 sorties in support of the army and casualties were heavy among the air crews.

Trooper J.W. Telford, 1st Battalion Royal Tank Regiment:

> Had about ten minutes sleep then bags of shelling and some Italian prisoners, they look stricken and utterly weary. Then a lull except for some very big guns further away. Then came news that the Greys and 5th tanks had got through. Then planes come over to do some bombing, one of A Squadrons tanks was hit by shelling. Then at 11:00 a.m. we are to have a daylight go at getting through the minefields. Only tried it once, A Squadron leading, lost five tanks on mines with Itie infantry on hand to shoot up the crews. Then news that the 4th CLY and 1/5th Queens were catching a packet, all rather apprehensive. We are to remain here but the advance seems to have petered out rather. The BBC says we are hanging on to our gains, we say what gains. Now they say things have gone well, watched tank buster Hurricanes in action near Himeimat.[28]

28 Manuscript sent to author by J.W. Telford 1992.

8

50th Northumbrian Division Attacks the Munassib Depression 25th October 1942

69th Brigade

The Munassib Depression was held by the formidable Italian paratroopers of the Folgore Division who had built strong defensive networks of minefields, booby trapped wire entanglements and mutually supporting strong points with clear fields of fire. The whole area and the surrounding desert had been zeroed in by their artillery and mortar crews in the rear and fire could be called down at will at any point should they be attacked. This feature was of an irregular shape, similar to an old weather beaten dried up riverbed. Its high sides were steep and dropped sharply to below the level of the surrounding desert. The paratroopers had concealed their defensive positions well and along the lip of the feature was a vast network of first line defences manned by resolute and determined defenders.

The 1st Greek Brigade had opposite their centre front the 20th Regiment of the Italian Brescia Division, to their left front was the German Burkhardt Parachute Battalion, Ramcke Brigade, and to their right front was the German Schweiger Parachute Battalion, Ramcke Brigade. Greek patrols were out constantly probing the enemy lines to gain information on the location of their positions and the strength of the forces they faced. Orders were received on 22nd October that the Greeks would make an attack between 22:00 p.m. and 24:00 p.m. on the 23rd October to gather information and cause confusion in the enemy ranks. This was to be a battle of attrition.

On the night of the 23rd October, as the barrage thundered along the entire Alamein line, the 1st Greek Brigade prepared to make a large scale raid into enemy territory led by the 4th Company of the 2nd Battalion which had been reinforced by two extra rifle platoons and a unit of engineers. The 1st Greek Regiment Field artillery would provide the barrage that covered the assault. The Greek units passed through their own wire as the barrage opened up in the early hours of 24th October, the attacking force moved as close to the barrage as they dare and when it stopped they attacked taking numerous

A lone Italian sentry looks out over the Munassib Depression. It was over this daunting landscape that 69 Brigade would have to launch their attack.(Author's collection)

Greek machine-gunners prepare for action.(Author's collection)

Italian positions in the first rush, many of the defenders were killed in the fighting and 18 Italian prisoners were taken. When the Greeks withdrew they had casualties of one dead and six wounded.

Clashes continued in no-man's land as Greek and enemy patrols seeking to gain dominance fought it out resulting in casualties to both sides. On the afternoon of 24th October the Greeks were about to make another attack in depth on the enemy lines when it was postponed, new orders arrived that this raid would be carried out on 25th October in support of the assault by 69 Brigade on the Munassib Depression. The Greek force was led by Captain Demosthenis Karavelas and consisted of the 4th Company, 1st Battalion, reinforced by two extra infantry platoons of the 2nd Company and a force of carriers. The attack went in under cover of a barrage near mid-night on 25th and many enemy positions were taken. This time they were faced not with Italians but the hardened and well organised paratroopers of the German Ramcke Brigade who counter-attacked in force. Mortar bombs rained down on the Greek attackers and heavy machine-gun fire raked the battle area. The violence of the German counter-attack forced the Greeks to give ground until they were left with the choice of destruction or retreat, they sensibly chose the latter and left their wounded and dead behind them.

In an attempt to relieve the pressure on 44th Division's front, XIII Corps issued orders on the morning of the 25th October that 69 Brigade was to attack features called the Cape and the Moor on the Munassib Depression that night. Supporting fire was to be given by the tanks of the 4th Armoured Brigade that had taken up a position just to the south of 69 Brigade.

Paratroopers of Burkhardt Parachute Battalion, Ramcke Parachute Brigade, recently out of action, share cigarettes with comrades. (Author's collection)

Throughout the day on 25th the Moor was subjected to continuous heavy artillery fire, at 22:30 p.m. an artillery smoke screen was put down to cover the advancing troops of the 6th Battalion Green Howards as they moved to their start line, which they crossed on time at 23:00 p.m. The leading companies of the 6th Battalion were B and C Companies with A Company and the carriers in reserve. As they approached the enemy wire one man from each platoon attached a grappling iron on a long rope to the wire, when the ropes were pulled by the carriers in unison the wire was torn up setting off numerous booby traps. The defences were breached and the 6th Battalion Green Howards advanced rapidly into the enemy positions held by the Italian Folgore Division. This alerted the enemy who immediately put down a storm of mortar and machine-gun fire. With bayonets fixed the 6th Green Howards ran across the minefield to assault the enemy forward positions. Ascending a crest they were met with more machine-gun fire from a second defensive line and Lt Herbert Livingstone Cull was killed along with several men of 13 platoon. Lt Dimond was at the head of 15 Platoon on the extreme right, they had missed the heaviest of the machine-gun fire and were making considerable progress. The scene was brightly lit by a full moon and they were spotted by the enemy who immediately engaged them in a fierce fire fight, Lt Dimond was wounded and his platoon suffered very heavy casualties.

Tommies take cover as enemy artillery fire falls before and around them. (Courtesy of Harry Forth)

An anonymous account has been left by an Italian paratrooper of the assault of the Green Howards and the bravery they showed:

> We were not able to see anything as our visibility was hampered by the huge black clouds produced by the smokescreen. I recall that all of a sudden one of the sentries emerged from his outpost and ran back towards the main trench. He was badly wounded, but he alerted the platoon of the impending British attack. The captain ordered six of us to start firing our Breda 38 machine-guns, while the remaining soldiers of the platoon were responsible for supplying us with the ammunition clips. The British ran toward us and tried to surround our firing point, but our machine-guns kept them away. These valiant soldiers came in waves one after the other. Each wave was cut down by our fire, but they continued to press on and eventually as the night battle wore on, our guns were silenced.[1]

17 Honey tanks supported the attack and nine of them were lost to accurate Italian anti-tank fire, they blazed fiercely on the battlefield.

Honey light tanks throw up dust clouds as they move off to the attack. (Author's collection)

1 P. Morisi, *The Italian Folgore Parachute Division* (Solihull: Helion and Company, 2016) p. 150.

Cpl William Francis Vickers MM, 6th Battalion Green Howards, C Coy, was with the forward platoon as they advanced:

> As 13 Platoon moved forward, led by Lt Dimond, the barrage ahead of us was thundering away and our objective, the Moor, got a good plastering. Smoke was laid down in front of us to give us some cover but as we passed through their minefield and wire entanglements we came under heavy fire from a number of Gerry machine-gun posts, the man next to me went down with the first burst. To add to the chaos Gerry started to drop mortar bombs and shells among us and we got pinned down as the fire was so intense. We lost most of the platoon there. We dived into slit trenches dug by the enemy, one lad called Joe Dolan got into one trench and it had been used by the Italians as a toilet for about four months. The excrement had dried so there was a thick crust on the top of it. When Joe realised what he had got into he started to scramble out of it and broke the crust, he was covered in shit from head to foot. When he finally got out he stood waving his fists towards the enemy and walked to the rear to get cleaned up. Bullets were whistling by and mortar and artillery shells were dropping all around him, but none hit him, he was so mad he ignored everything. Later on we saw him and said, 'shit for luck Joe but you'll survive'. But he was killed in Sicily in 1943, he came to us with a draft of Cameron Highlanders.[2]

Cpl William Francis Vickers MM, 6th Battalion Green Howards. (Courtesy of William Francis Vickers, MM)

2 Interview with author, William Francis Vickers. 1990.

Major Pullinger then led B Company up to the high ground but was also held up by the heavy machine-gun fire from both flanks, this was soon intensified by mortar and artillery fire and the situation became critical. Major Pullinger steadied his company and led them with pistol in hand in one last ditch bayonet charge on to the Moor in a bid to save the situation. B Company ran forward hurling grenades into the enemy posts, killing the gunners with bayonet and shot in a desperate close quarter encounter, just after midnight they had captured one third of the Moor and began to consolidate their own positions. Major Pullinger went on to contact C Company on the right flank under heavy shell-fire and found them pinned to the ground with their commander dead. He re-organised them and led them in a successful attack onto their own objective, taking 70 prisoners in the process. For his courage and leadership he was awarded the Military Cross for this action. Casualties for the 6th Green Howards in this attack had been over 100 so far.

Bofors gun team in action. (Author's collection)

The Folgore War Diary observed:

> It was a particularly fierce enemy assault. Enemy units under cover of a smokescreen managed to infiltrate the stronghold. Its advanced firing points were quickly surrounded by infantry. These units crashed into the positions situated in the resistance zone leading to two hours of very intense fighting. One by one our anti-tank units ran out of ammunition and could not be re-supplied as they had been completely cut off from the other strong points. At

> that point one by one of our automatic weapons units were also put out of action by the tanks. At 04:00 a.m. only a few firing points were still standing, while Captain Constantino Ruspoli had fallen, killed by machine-gun fire.[3]

The 6th Battalion Green Howards Headquarters had taken several direct hits while this action was being fought and Major Faye, 2 I/C, Captain G.S. Piper, Adjutant, and a number of headquarters staff had been seriously injured. Lt Honneyman organised the extricating of the wounded to the nearest casualty clearing station. The commander of the 6th Battalion, Lt Colonel Lance, ordered a section of bren-gun carriers up through the minefield gap cleared by the engineers. The first carrier went through only to detonate a mine and burst into flames, the engineers had to go back into the minefield with their detectors and begin to clear another gap through the area already passed through by the leading companies. As the sappers worked a mine exploded killing and wounding a number of them, shells and mortar bombs were exploding all around them and at first it was assumed that they had taken a direct hit. The detectors were dispensed with and the men began the old tried and tested method of prodding the ground with their 18 inch bayonets, this brought immediate results and a number of wooden cased mines were unearthed. These mines could not be located by a detector which could only find metal objects. It was found out later that the area between the two belts of wire was strewn with this new type of mine and it was only by luck that the two attacking companies had not set them off as they advanced over them.

Lt Colonel Lance arrived at the front line and was told of the precarious position of C Company, at 01:40 a.m. he ordered the reserve, A Company and carriers, to launch an attack on the enemy strongpoints that were still holding out on the Moor. C Company was held up by heavy shell-fire and Captain Edwards killed as the carriers attacked a well dug-in strongpoint, 35 prisoners were taken when the strong point fell. Many casualties were taken in this vicious close quarter fighting and numerous acts of gallantry were performed as men risked, and often gave, their lives to press home the attack. By 02:30 a.m. on 26th October the 6th Green Howards were firmly established on Point 94 and were strengthened by the arrival of anti-tank and machine-gun sections. As they consolidated their positions mortar fire and artillery fire swept the area continuously. A further attack across the Moor to Point 192 was planned and at 02:30 a.m. artillery fire and a smoke screen from the mortars fell on Point 192. A Company advanced over the bullet swept plateau and as they approached Point 192 the enemy laid down a tremendous artillery barrage that caused the attack to falter. The paratroopers of the Folgore Division formed up and counter-attacked

3 P. Morisi, *The Italian Folgore Parachute Division* (Solihull.: Helion and Company, 2016] p. 151.

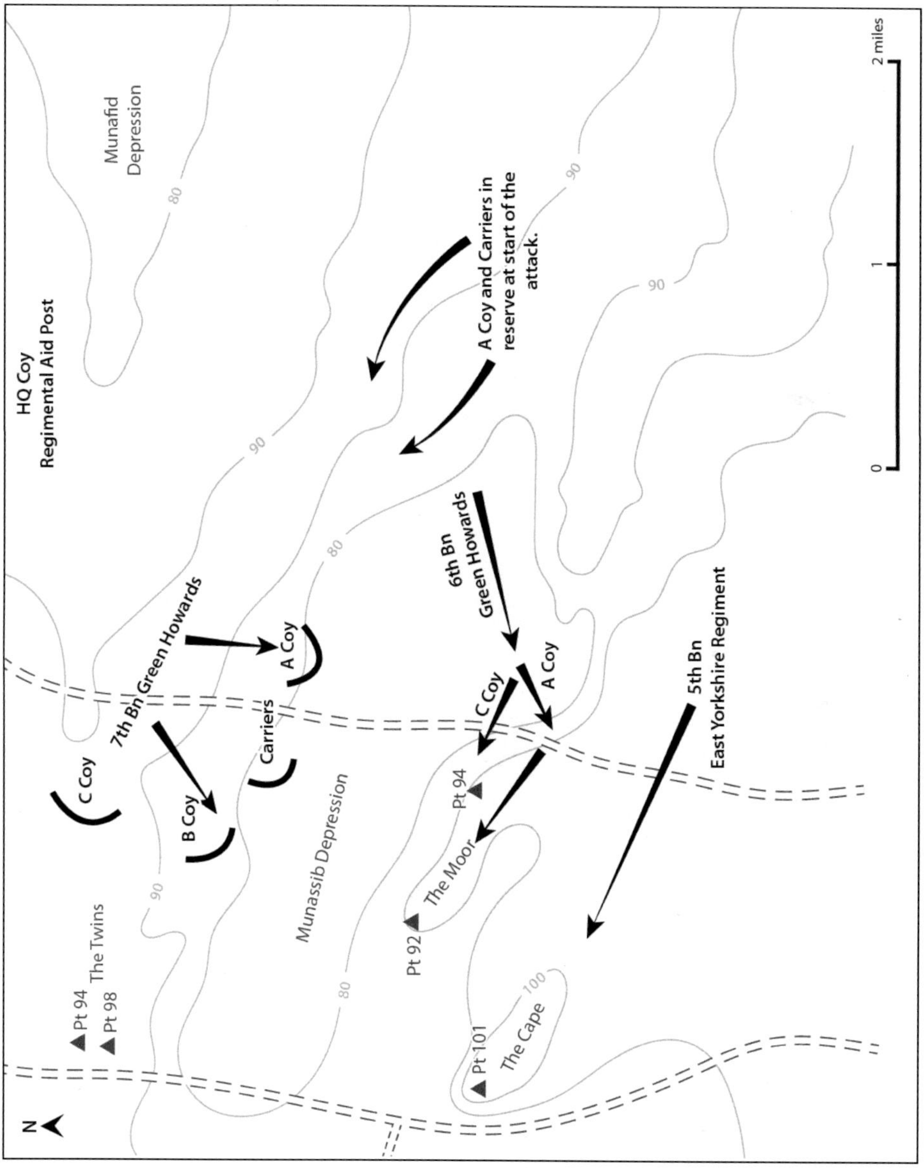

The 50th Northumbrian Division attacks the Munassib Depression, 25th October 1942.

Sappers working to clear mines whilst under fire. (Author's collection)

Lt Colonel Dereck Anthony Seagrim VC, CO 7th Battalion Green Howards. Killed in action at the Battle of the Wadi Akarit, 6th April 1943. (Author's collection)

both flanks of the advancing British troops and fought a fierce close combat encounter whilst keeping up a hail of machine-gun fire from concealed positions, causing heavy casualties in A Company. Lt Gray was missing and Captain Walker was seriously wounded. By 03:00 a.m. a badly shaken A Company was down to one third of its original strength and orders were received to retire leaving many of their wounded behind. After almost super human efforts and after nearly 200 casualties the 6th Battalion held part of the Moor but failed to reach all of their objectives.

The 7th Battalion Green Howards, under the command of Lt Colonel Dereck Anthony Seagrim, was situated in a rough semi-circle on the northern escarpment of the Munassib Depression. C Company had to its front Points 194 and 198, known as the twins to the troops. They were strongly held by the paratroopers of the Italian Folgore Division.

Company Sergeant Major Jack Verity, 7th Battalion Green Howards, was with C Company:

> Patrolling was going on by all our companies and the enemy, they often clashed, and we could hear the noise, mainly at night, as fire fights took place. Every day we would get the 'morning hate' from Gerry, this was an artillery bombardment that took place at a regular time and lasted for about 15 minutes usually. Early one morning the order came down that we were to engage all enemy positions with machine-guns and mortars, Gerry soon replied, and mortar bombs started to thud around us causing casualties. Salvoes of bombs were crashing down on us for quite a while. At one point a sandstorm blew across the whole area followed by rain, making things even more miserable. Gerry put down a ferocious barrage of shell, mortar and

Company Sergeant Major Jack Verity, 7th Battalion Green Howards. (Courtesy of Jack Verity)

> machine-gun fire on the whole of the battalion area, the order to 'stand to' was given but no counter-attack came, much to our relief. One patrol brought in a prisoner, a member of the 185th Regiment, Italian Folgore Parachute Division, he was sent to the rear for questioning. The shelling of our positions increased on the 25th as the whole area was swept with fire morning, noon and night, making any movement virtually impossible. On the 26th we had a grandstand view of the attack by the 6th Battalion on the Moor. We kept up a constant supporting fire on the enemy positions, harassed all the while by enemy shell and mortar fire.[4]

Pte Ted Lowthorpe, 7th Battalion Green Howards, recalls the heavy mortar fire that fell upon his position:

Pte Ted Lowthorpe, 7th Battalion Green Howards. (Courtesy of Ted Lowthorpe)

> There was a terrific explosion that knocked me sideways and took off both of my mate Chalkie White's legs. He stared at me with an astonished look on his face and I went to help him, he pointed at the raw bleeding stump of one leg with the white bone sticking through. Just then a machine-gun opened up and poor old Chalkie got it full in the face. Tracer bullets flew towards us and then there was another tremendous crash and I was knocked unconscious for a short while, when I came to the mortar bombs were still falling around us.[5]

4 Interview with author. Jack Verity, Beverley 1989.
5 Ibid., Ted Lowthorpe Hull 1991.

On the left flank of the Green Howards the 5th Battalion East Yorkshire Regiment prepared to make their assault on the Cape. This was a strongly fortified position occupied by a Young Fascist Battalion of the Italian Folgore Parachute Division. On the night of the 25th October the attacking companies of the 5th Battalion moved to their start line without too much trouble, but this was to be the lull before the storm. A creeping barrage was laid down before the advancing troops and they had to keep as close to it as they could. The Italians crouched in their dug-outs until the British barrage had passed over them. The East Yorkshiremen reached the minefield wire without incident, the Italian defenders had allowed them to get closer in order to draw them into a trap, waiting quietly anti-tank gun crews, mortar teams and machine gunners watched as some of the attackers began to move through the minefield and into the Italian positions. When the British were only 200 yards from the Italian outposts the paratroopers opened fire, pushing back the forward companies. Bren carriers carried grappling hooks with which to tear down the minefield wire and set off booby traps, the first four to reach the minefields were hit by accurate anti-tank fire and others exploded as they ran onto mines. This left only one carrier which cleared a small amount of wire then ran onto a mine. Artillery support was signalled for but when the shells arrived they landed on top of the 5th Battalion's positions.

Men of the Young Fascist Battalion, Italian Folgore Parachute Division on the Munassib Depression. (Author's collection)

Pte Jim Betts, 5th Battalion East Yorkshire Regiment, advanced with A Company on the left of the attack:

> We all got a tot of rum each and went in at 11 at night, one of the new replacements said to me 'I won't be coming back' and I said, 'don't be daft', that was the last I saw of him. We had this carrier going up with us, rolling across the desert in the middle of the night and there was this terrible creeping barrage, it was frightening, a creeping barrage. I've never known anything like it in my life and it was creeping slowly in front of us as we were going in, what a deafening noise it made. We got to this wire and the carrier was supposed to pull it down with grappling hooks. The first thing they hit was this carrier, it was like daylight when it blew up and we all dived to the floor. Mortar bombs and all sorts were going off around us, we got so far past this minefield when somebody on our left sent up a rocket for artillery support, the shells came down on us instead of on Gerry and it was murder. We were told to get out if we could, so we pulled back a bit and bumped into another company who asked us what we were doing there. We told the officer our orders were to get out, he said 'no get back and use your bayonets', he got us a carrier and the sergeant driving it took us forward and said 'we can't get through here so do as you like' and dropped us off in the middle of all this chaos.[6]

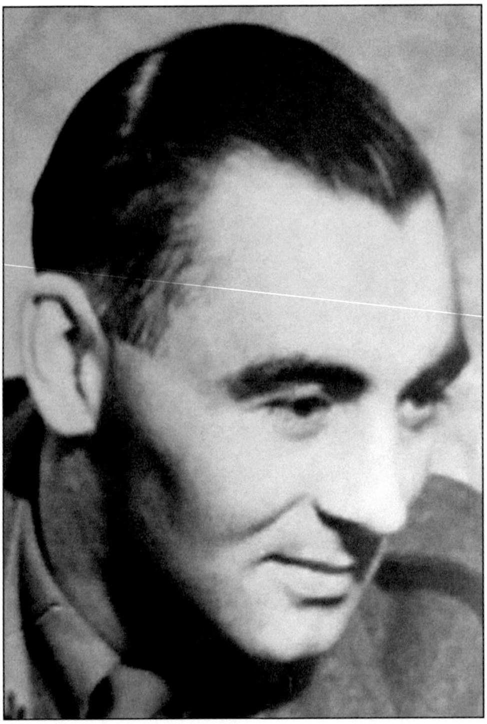

Pte Jim Betts, 5th Battalion East Yorkshire Regiment. (Courtesy of Jim Betts)

6 Interview with author. Jim Betts Hull 1992.

Sergeant William Thompson, 5th Battalion East Yorkshire Regiment, advanced with A Company and recalls the fierce confusion of battle:

> Being in battle was a bloody frightening thing, you could see tracer bullets coming straight at you and they would pass you with a sharp wack. The barrage was like being in a loud scary thunderstorm and when we set off we couldn't see a thing, sand and smoke clouds were everywhere and shells whistled overhead. I can't tell you, kids got killed alongside you, men hit would fall without a sound, we had to leave the wounded behind in the hope that they would be picked up by the medics.[7]

Sergeant William Thompson, 5th Battalion East Yorkshire Regiment. (Courtesy of William Thompson)

The situation of was serious enough to be mentioned in the regimental war diary. Many men were hit by this friendly fire and the 5th Battalion had to pull back to escape their own barrage. Wireless communication was lost with battalion headquarters and runners had to take messages through the fire that was sweeping the area. In the ensuing chaos over 150 casualties had been taken during the attack and the only chance of success now was to send a fresh company into the fray with a heavy artillery bombardment going before them. However dawn was approaching leaving insufficient time to organise a renewed attack and the 5th Battalion East Yorkshire Regiment was ordered to withdraw to a defensive position from which they could keep up a harassing fire on the enemy lines, they were in position as dawn broke. The aborted attack on the Cape had been a costly exersize with little to show for the sacrifice and General Nichols decided to call a halt to the attacks.

7 Ibid., William Thompson, Beverley 1993.

9

151st Brigade

The 151st Brigade had been patrolling aggressively in the days prior to 22nd October but no patrols went out on the 22nd as the 9th Battalion Durham Light Infantry prepared for a raid on the evening of the 23rd. The objective was to identify the enemy units opposing them, to destroy any enemy weapons they came across and to make two lanes through the minefields and barbed wire so they could be used the following night. The raid was to be led by Lt Wilkes, it was made up of 24 other ranks from A Company and four sappers from the 505th Field Coy, Royal Engineers, equipped with Bangalore Torpedoes to clear the barbed wire entanglements. The raiding party left their own lines at midnight on the 23rd, they could see and hear clearly the British barrage that was flashing and thundering all along the line. As they advanced to the enemy wire without any incident they were spotted by enemy machine-gunners who opened up with a heavy concentration of small arms fire. Lt Wilkes and Lt Hutchinson were killed instantly and two other ranks were captured. The raiders withdrew under covering fire from a patrol from C Company who were based on the edge of the German minefield, no more casualties were taken.

Sapper John F Mathews, 505th Field Coy, Royal Engineers was one of the raiders:

> I was sent on detachment to the 9th DLI and we went out on a raid, the officer went forward and was shot dead almost immediately [Lt Wilkes] and the sergeant took command. He told us to get down which we did and heavy firing followed, the man next to me had been shot through the wrist. The sergeant shouted 'get out of it boys' and the enemy shouted for us to surrender, the private next to me got up with me and we ran being followed by tracer bullets all the time, I was wearing new army boots and couldn't run well at all, it was like a bad dream. We found a slit trench and fell into it as the enemy started putting up flares which lit up the whole area. I bandaged the private's hand with a field dressing and as soon as the coast was clear we headed for our own lines.[1]

1 Manuscript sent to author by John F. Mathews Leeds 1991.

The much feared German Mark IV Special. (Author's collection)

The failure of 44th Division and 7th Armoured Division to reach their objectives brought about a change of plan for 151 Brigade. Their purpose now was to attack Points 98 and 94 from the east and the plan was dependent upon the attack of the 69 Brigade on the Cape and the Moor being successful.

On the night of the 26th October B company of the 9th Battalion Durham Light Infantry was to carry out a raid to test the strength of the enemy positions north of the Munassib Depression, Lt W S (Scotty) White led 11 Platoon:

> To begin with at Alamein we were faced by the Italian Folgore Parachute Division, they were tough nuts, all the things you hear about the Italians running away didn't apply to the Folgore and we respected them. We were given the task of neutralising an isolated position held by the Folgore. On the evening of the 23rd our company was to go to a taped start line and part of the 7th Armoured Division was to advance to a place behind the strongpoint. Immediately they got behind the hill the code word Chicken would be passed over the wireless and we on the start line would charge up the hill, through mines and wire and all. My platoon was to lead the charge, we walked out on to the tape and lay down. If the wire hadn't been cut by the artillery I was to fling myself on top of it and the rest of the platoon likewise and the following platoons were to run over the top of us, I thought that's a nice to do. I had no

A German tank delivers fuel to the front. (Author's collection)

Troops and tanks moving forward over a flat featureless landscape. (Courtesy of Max Hearst)

> sense of this being a foolhardy affair and within minutes of getting there we got the code word Goose which meant it was off.[2]

This operation was moved to the following night but was again cancelled, the men of the DLI were by now suffering from a combination of physical exhaustion, lack of sleep and intense stress.

The whole of the operation in the south was now halted on Montgomery's orders. They had served their main purpose, which was to keep the two enemy armoured divisions in the south as long as possible so they could not interfere with the main area of attack in the northern sector. The enemy in the south still sat on top of Mount Himeimat, giving them full observation of all that was happening on the sandy plane below. On 26th October Rommel issued orders that the 21st Panzer Division and one third of the Ariete Division battle group should be moved north to reinforce 15th Panzer and Littorio Division's sector. The official history of the period estimates that XIII Corps, from the 23rd to 26th October, sustained a total of 1,040 casualties.

2 H. Moses, *The Gateshead Gurkha* (Durham: County Durham Books, 2001), p. 201.

10

Operation on the Snipe: Northern Sector 26th – 27th October 1942

Montgomery's new offensive in the north began in late October as the Australian Division made a thrust for the coast cutting off the German 164th Light Division, the reaction from the Afrika Korps was fierce in the extreme and they launched determined counter-attacks. This prevented the Australians from reaching the coast, they were only able to take the coast road and railway and here they hung on tenaciously despite everything the axis units threw at them. Rommel needed desperately to dislodge them and some of the most savage fighting in the battle now occurred. The fight flowed back and forth as positions were taken, lost and retaken again and again. For four days the Australians held on, refusing to give ground in the face of numerous armoured assaults, in four days they suffered 5,000 casualties while beating off the enemy. They drew on to their front the greater part of the axis armoured units and destroyed a large part of them with their well sited and dug-in anti-tank guns.

On 26th and 27th October the 1st Armoured Division was plunged into some of the stiffest fighting of the battle so far. On 26th they embarked upon an operation that ran headlong into a massive counter attack by Rommel's forces and they proved again that a well manned anti-tank gun screen could repulse enemy armour with heavy losses. Their positions were hastily occupied and devoid of any natural advantage and though minefields were constantly being laid it was now mainly the anti-tank gun that was halting the Axis armour. Two enemy fortified positions were now to be attacked at night with mortorised infantry and from these firm bases the armoured brigades would thrust westward. One of these localities had been shown by aerial photographs to be strengthened with heavy wire entanglements and gun positions and it was known by the code-word Woodcock, it was situated north-west of Kidney Ridge. The second, code named Snipe, was less heavily defended and was situated a mile further south. The Snipe was to be attacked by the 2nd Battalion Rifle Brigade and Woodcock would be attacked by 2nd Battalion King's Royal Rifle Corps. Both of these operations

Anti-tank gunners crouch low behind the protection of their gun shield as they wait for the enemy armour to come into killing range. (Author's collection)

A British six pounder anti-tank gun team ready for action. (Courtesy of Roy Walker)

would be supported by the massed artillery of X and XXX Corps and at dawn on 27th the 2nd Armoured Brigade would move forward to the Snipe and 24th Armoured Brigade to Woodcock. At 23:00 p.m. on the night of the 26th October the attack on Woodcock went in, the 2nd Battalion King's Royal Rifle Corps accompanied by 76th Anti-tank Regiment advanced into clouds of dust thrown up by the artillery barrage and by its own Bren-carriers which preceded the soldiers on foot. This caused great difficulty in keeping direction to their objective as they moved through thick shadowy clouds of dust and noise. They found little opposition and when the barrage stopped they formed a defensive position. When daylight came they realised they were in an exposed position south of Woodcock and that to stay there through the day would be to invite disaster. The fog of war had been complete, the attack had missed its mark and they withdrew quickly to a more secure position.

The 2nd Battalion Rifle Brigade and the 239th Anti-tank Battery advanced through minefields in the direction of the Snipe at 23:00 p.m. on 26th October over a featureless terrain. They would have to make a dash through enemy held country and establish an island of resistance. Here they would hold on until the arrival of 24th Armoured Brigade the next day. They were to follow the creeping barrage that would thunder before them and lead them onto their objective. By 23:00 p.m. the barrage was in full swing, throwing up the usual fog that the men and machines would have to advance through, carriers, infantry and sappers. For the first 1,000 yards there was a little fire coming their way but no opposition on the ground. Pauses were inevitable as wire entanglements were found and the sappers moved in to test for mines. A group of German engineers was seen on route, some ran away but 20 gave themselves up without resistance.

Lt Colonel Vic Turner, VC, OC 2nd Battalion Rifle Brigade, remembers the chaotic start to the operation:

> We were all in position and Z minus 5 arrived and with it the artillery concentration, but did it go down on a bearing of 233 degrees? Not on your life, it was on a bearing of 275 degrees! This meant forming up again on a new bearing and re-setting our compasses, a by no means easy task by the light of a just rising moon. We left the start line at 23:00 p.m. with my company commanders each mounted in a wireless carrier and I in a wireless jeep driven by Major Tom Bird. Our start was anything but auspicious as we drove straight into a German vehicle pit within a hundred yards. However there was no danger and we got a carrier to pull us out. There was a certain amount of AP tracer and MG bullets flying about but nothing serious. On the right we could see a good deal of fire in the north from the Woodcock direction.[1]

1 D. Lee, *Up Close and Personal* (Barnsley: Frontline Books, 2015), p. 123.

Rifleman H. Suckling, 2nd Battalion Rifle Brigade, recalls the confusion as he advanced in a Bren-carrier:

> Our carriers were advancing firing their light machine-guns at targets or at anything on our front. We didn't realise what was coming at us because of the constant noise, we only thought of what was hitting the enemy. We'd have a quick look at targets then give it a quick burst just to reassure ourselves. When we passed slit trenches it was a quick pull of the hand-grenade pin and in with it, in the hope that you would knock some of them out. We didn't wait to see if there was anybody in them as the line was moving on in the advance. It was a rather flat area and there was no good cover only some camel shrub, once behind a bit of that and it seemed like an oak tree and any small mound seemed like a hill.[2]

Sgt Joe Swann, DCM, 2nd Battalion Rifle Brigade:

> The only way we could keep in line was by heading into the thickest of the dust. The officers had gone ahead with the colonel and we just pushed on behind. It was awful because there was so much muck being thrown up into the air that you just couldn't see anything. We experienced that all the time in the desert. The road and the sky was clear but if you was at the back you got all their dust. We opened up our anti-gas stuff and put the visors on so we could continue to see.[3]

It was thought that the barrage was going too far and the advance was halted, in fact they never reached their original map reference for the Snipe but ended up 900 yards short of it. Verey lights went up indicating success just past midnight and the anti-tank guns were then ordered forward, the soft sand hindered their progress but by 03:45 a.m. most were up with the infantry who had by now dug-in in their allotted sectors. Telephone lines were run out between the companies, the ground was rotten with excreta and a few dead Germans lay about in the sand.

Cpt F.W. Marten, MC, remembers the new position they had found as being heaven sent:

> The colonel said stop and I said to him 'Have we come to the right place?' He said 'I don't know but this is where we are and here we stay'. By great good fortune he had found this place and I had found this dug-out which could

2 Letter to author from H Suckling 1993.
3 Ibid., J Swann 1989.

A fallen position littered with dead soldiers and their abandoned equipment. (Author's collection)

> house me, the signallers and the wireless sets. It was twelve feet long by six feet wide, quite deep. There were some steps and the roof was covered with railway sleepers. We were in a heaven sent position because we were in a very shallow disc, I suppose it only went down about two or three feet and was covered in scrub and old bits of engineering stores. It meant that as soon as we were dug-in an enemy approaching couldn't see any trace of our occupation. The guns were dug in more or less in a circular ring as decided by Vic Turner and Tom Bird. In between them were the riflemen and Bren guns.[4]

The dust settled and a bright moon appeared in the sky, carriers reconnoitred the surrounding landscape and skirmished with the enemy more than once. A mixed force of enemy tanks, self-propelled guns and vehicles was not too far away and at 03:45 a.m. the roar of tank engines was heard and dark shapes could be seen moving about and advancing towards the British outpost. The anti-tank gunners made ready and sat behind their six pounder guns waiting for the tanks to come within range. A big Mark IV panzer came to within 30 yards of C Company and the first shot struck the tank which then burst into flames. A Company then shot up a self-propelled gun which proceeded to brew up nicely.

Sgt Joe Swann, anti-tank platoon, A Company, 2nd Battalion the Rifle Brigade, saw the enemy armour approach:

4 Manuscript sent to author by F.W. Marten 1989.

> A tank was about 150 yards away and I took a bang at him and stopped him. With the next shot I jammed his turret and the next shot I put into his side and couple of blokes jumped out. One bloke was trapped inside for about eight hours screaming for help. [The screams of agony could be heard though-out the position for the rest of the day until mercifully he died][5]

Rifleman H. Suckling and his mates were very grateful to Sergeant Swann though the good Sergeant never knew it:

> Round about this time I glanced back behind me and to the right rear was a Panzer 1V, I told the lads to keep their heads down. Out front there was quite a lot of movement of vehicles but our thoughts were concentrated on the tank in our rear. We knew there was a six pounder anti-tank gun to our right facing front but there was no fire coming from it and we assumed the crew were knocked out or out of ammo. If one of us crawled to it perhaps we could have a go at the panzer, we did a John Wayne and raised a tin hat above our slit trench. The tank gave it a burst from his MG, it would have been suicide for any of us to get out and have a go. All of a sudden there was an explosion over our position and we thought it was the tank firing at us with his 75mm. Deeper down we crouched into our trench. Then there was a pall of smoke and the smell of burning rubber, we looked over the edge of our trench and the panzer was burning. This was the tank that Sergeant Swann knocked out and we didn't know this at the time but what a relief it was.[6]

Swann adjusted the position of his gun and as he did so a new target came into view:

> I was just moving the gun into position when a 7.62 mm self-propelled gun came across our front 200 yards away. There was a road going round the escarpment and this gun was up there firing at us. Colonel Vic Turner, the commanding officer, was at our gun at the time and said to me 'Swann do you think you can hit it. I said 'I'll have a go'. I swivelled the gun round and laid it onto a butt in the bank so that the nose of the vehicle, as it came into it, would give me the cue to fire, so I fired at it and hit it. When it was stationary I put another one into it and the people inside bowled out of it and disappeared. So that stopped that one.[7]

5 Interview with author J. Swann 1989.

6 Manuscript sent to author by H. Suckling 1992.

7 Letter to author from J. Swann 1990.

A German tank passing a knocked out British Bren-carrier. (Courtesy of Norman Hardy)

The rest of the enemy force then turned away as the sky turned light grey, some of them taking cover in folds in the ground only a few hundred yards to the west of the Rifle Brigade. Only one crewman escaped from the Mark IV that had been knocked out and he sniped at the British positions all night. At first light a rifleman went out to find his location and killed him with a grenade. The infantry that had watched events unfold were jubilant, firing the men with a new optimism and confidence which would grow as the battle developed.

A bitterly cold wind whipped across this inhospitable landscape as the officers got their bearings, the scene they looked out over was almost flat with faint folds in the desert for a mile and a half all around the shallow oval British position. The infantry, sappers and anti-tank gunners sat tight in their gun-pits and trenches. When daylight finally came it would be the excellence of their digging and concealment that would save them from taking unnecessary casualties. In the grey daylight the panzers began to move away from the Snipe going about their allotted tasks for the day, a number of them which had taken cover in dead-ground for the night broke cover about 700 yards away and presented a tempting target to the anti-tank gunners watching. The morning light was shattered as numerous anti-tank guns opened fire into the flanks and rear of the German tanks. A large number of tanks and self-propelled guns were destroyed in a spectacular show of fire-power and marksmanship and the German crews who bailed out were shot down by machine-gun fire. Cheers rang out from the British trenches at this display of aggression but now the location of the position was disclosed to the enemy and the Snipe was heavily shelled as gun teams began to move to more favourable gun-pits, this movement attracted even more shell-fire. Hiding in the centre of the British position was an unarmed German soldier who stood up and ran for his life, the Tommies never fired at him and let him go.

Rifleman Edward Blacker, sniper, 2nd Rifle Brigade, spent most of his time in the battle taking pot-shots at the enemy machine gunners and snipers:

> From where I was I could see German tanks everywhere. There was one that came within eight yards of where I was, I kept dead quiet and dead still. It was so close to me that the soft sand as it turned poured over me. I was mainly going after the snipers and machine-guns and that was a simple job as I could pick them off. They were sitting up firing their machine-guns and there were some blokes shooting grenades at them. People say there wasn't a lot of infantry at the Snipe but there was. The sun was up bright and hot and some of the snipers were lying on tanks, it was hard to see these snipers because they might be hidden by all the stuff rolled up on top of the tanks. A lot of these snipers were getting away with it but nobody knew I was there and that was a disaster for them. I had everything my way and had no worries about getting hit, I knew they didn't know where I was.[8]

Rifleman H Suckling:

> There was light machine-gun and rifle fire and heavy stuff flying everywhere and big clouds of black smoke from knocked out vehicles and tanks. Our anti-tank guns were doing their stuff, without them we would have been useless. We could never have held out fighting with small arms alone. When Gerry came it was with tanks and mobile guns and our anti-tank gunners did good work with these, the six pounders stopped them cold. Then as the crews began to bale out and we opened up on them.[9]

Rifleman Edward Blacker and his mate were searching for C Company when he came across Sergeant Eldo Francise, anti-tank gunner, who was in a bit of a state as his gun was being sniped at from a knocked out German tank. There was a pop-pop as bullets hit the shield of his six pounder anti-tank gun, I said 'Where's C Company?' he said 'Never mind bloody C Company, see that tank down there, the two of you go

8 Manuscript sent to author from E. Blacker 1992.
9 Ibid., H. Suckling 1992.

German anti-tank gunners in action with blazing British tank in the distance. (Author's collection)

down and stop them sods from firing at us'. He asked how to get down there and the distraught sergeant yelled 'Use your bloody loaf':

> It took us a few minutes to crawl the 80 yards to the tank, it had been hit by a shell and looked as though it had been there for some time. When we got there we raked a lot of the soft sand out from under it with our hands and made ourselves a nice position underneath the tank by then it was starting to get light. We could see what was happening, there was one tank that had been hit by a shell but it hadn't burst into flames, the crew were still inside and were still firing. The firing had stopped and when they came out of the study Johnny said to me 'Shall we do it?' I said we should let them get a bit further away otherwise we might be spotted and find ourselves in trouble. So as they went we popped [killed] them, one got away but the other two had no chance, we were a bit soft on the third one.[10]

With full daylight the nakedness of the British position became all too obvious and to the south west could be seen the ominous shape of Hill 37, from here the German

10 Manuscript sent to author E Blacker 1992.

artillery spotters could direct their artillery fire onto the Snipe. At 07:30 a.m. the Tommies looked across the desert and saw a great cloud of dust approaching them, it was the tanks of the 24th Armoured Brigade who then halted to look for the British garrison. They saw a strongpoint 2,000 yards ahead and a number of knocked out and burning German tanks scattered about the desert. Not recognising it as their own point of manoeuvre they opened fire on their own side with high explosive shells. This was eventually stopped but it was galling to the Rifle Brigade, sappers and anti-tank gunners that had to suffer this friendly fire.

Lt Warwick, A Squadron, 47th Battalion, Royal Tank Regiment, advanced through the enemy minefield and was held up by heavy shell-fire:

> We replied to this fire until ordered to advance south-west for almost a mile. During this advance I was on the right flank and in touch with a battalion of the Rifle Brigade who were holding a position on the slopes of Kidney Hill. Several of our tanks on my left opened fire on these friends killing several. I screamed over the air to stop this with little or no effect.[11]

At 07:30 a.m. Lt Colonel Vic Turner, VC, OC 2nd Battalion Rifle Brigade, heard the sound of tanks approaching from the east:

> Shermans of the 24th Armoured Brigade appeared on a ridge 2,000 yards east of the Snipe and started to shell us vigorously with 75mm high explosive and machine-gun fire. There was really some excuse for it as we were surrounded by derelict enemy tanks and self-propelled guns and they themselves were being heavily shelled by 88mm guns. I sent Lt Wintour off in a carrier to meet 24th Armoured Brigade. He found the leading squadron commander and said 'Look here, you're shelling our position.' 'I'm awfully sorry' the squadron commander said. 'Not half as sorry as we are' replied Jackie Wintour. The leading squadron stopped shooting but not so the remainder of the brigade, who continued to roar us up until about 25 tanks started forming up about 1,500 yards to our south and south-west, when the armoured brigade began to realise who were the real enemy.[12]

At 08:00 a.m. the 24th Armoured Brigade began their advance to the Snipe and as they did so 25 German tanks of the newest and most powerful design took hull-down positions to the rear of Hill 37 waiting for the British tanks to come into firing range. In doing so they presented themselves as perfect targets to the anti-tank gunners on

11 Letter to the author from Mr Warwick 1990.

12 D. Lee, *Up Close and Personal* (Barnsley: Frontline Books, 2006), p. 141.

the Snipe and at a range of 1,100 yards they engaged the German tanks knocking three of them out immediately. As the crews bailed out the machine-gunners of the 24th Armoured Brigade mowed them down without mercy.

Sgt Douglas Covill DCM, 10th Hussars:

> On 27th October we were positioned near a ridge which overlooked the positions held by the Rifle Brigade. Our squadron was hull-down, which meant we were just below the ridge. I could see the whole area where the Rifle Brigade was being attacked, to the left and slightly obscured by our own ridge was the Snipe position. This meant that when the Germans came in we were in a good position to be able to shoot some of them up. The whole squadron was 15 tanks strong, each about 40 yards from the next and stung out in a line firing at the Germans. We fired a couple of hundred shells that day and I know we hit a number of enemy tanks, the tanks we couldn't hit got under the ridge and we could no longer take aim at them. The Rifle Brigade had to deal with these themselves.[13]

As the tanks of the 24th Armoured Brigade moved forward and joined forces with the garrison on the Snipe the enemy reacted violently, every weapon he had was brought to bear on the stationary Sherman tanks. The anti-tank guns of the 115th Panzer Grenadiers and 33rd Panzerjagers, panzers in hull-down positions and the heavy shells of the German medium artillery poured fire onto the British position. The whole area became an inferno of bursting high explosive shells, smoke and darting tracer rounds. Within 15 minutes seven Shermans were ablaze as the British tanks got the worst of the engagement.

Lt C H Hanna, A Squadron, 47th Battalion, Royal Tank Regiment, received orders that A Squadron was to advance under a smoke screen to the position held by the 2nd Rifle Brigade:

> As we came up onto the ridge we were under shell-fire and then anti-tank guns opened up from all around, some at less than 100 yards. Most of the time we did not know what was hitting us. At the same time as we were receiving hits on our front, a shot from the rear removed our right idler and another penetrated the rear of the engines. We managed to recover the tank but lost touch with the battalion. As we came out we were the target for every gun around and smoke would have been very useful. We were using the browning machine-gun at close range which put up enough dust to help, when we got a second separated ammunition case. This put the gun out of action as we had

13 Manuscript sent to author by H. Limer 1991.

> no tool for removing it and just had to use our spare barrel to clear a similar stoppage.[14]

Lt Fulton, 47th Battalion, Royal Tank Regiment, came under fire as his squadron moved towards the Rifle Brigade:

> When we were only 500 yards away and the position of the tanks was Cpt Crinks in Defiant on my left front, myself followed by the rest of the squadron. Arran and Defiant were hit almost at the same time in front, Lt Warwick just behind me. The spare driver of Arran and Corporal Munn was blown out of the tank and took cover. Defiant was on fire but still moving in reverse. I could not see the gun or guns which engaged us and withdrew about 100 yards to hull-down to try and spot him. We moved forward a bit to the left and came right on top of a Mark IV Special, it was firing across our front. We put three rounds of AP through it and had to withdraw again, but it had ceased firing and was smoking round the turret ring.[15]

Lt Warwick, 47th Battalion, Royal Tank Regiment:

> Two 88mm guns then opened up and knocked out three tanks almost immediately. This gun was on the right flank and although several tanks were behind me none of them registered or attempted to silence it. My co-driver was killed immediately as the right ammunition sponson was hit and exploded. The projectile then ricocheted around the floor of the turret killing the wireless operator and wounding the gunner.[16]

It was obvious that the armoured brigade could not stay in this death trap and they withdrew over a mile away to take up hull-down positions, the poor infantry were not sorry to see them go. As they did so the anti-tank gunners on the Snipe continued to take a steady toll of the German armour.

Lt Colonel Vic Turner, VC, OC Rifle Brigade, watched as the British tanks withdrew:

> The Shermans were engaged by tanks and guns from the north. It was at a Mark IV Special out of these tanks that 239 Battery had their first shoot. It was at extreme range but at 1,800 yards that it was halted at the third shot. Another tank immediately came up and towed it away. Shelled as we were by tanks and

14 Letter to author from C.H. Hanna 1993.
15 Ibid., Mr Fulton 1991.
16 Ibid., Mr Warwick 1990.

> guns we sent an R/T message to HQ crying out for an OP, the reply was that one would be sent shortly but he never arrived.[17]

Cpt F.W. Marten, MC, Rifle Brigade:

> During the day the fire was so intense on the Snipe and on the approaches to it, that no vehicles could get across to us. This had two serious consequences: the regimental medical officer was never able to get to us and we badly needed a doctor and secondly we became critically short of ammunition but couldn't get any more.[18]

By now the enemy had come to the conclusion that the Snipe position which was giving them so much trouble would have to be wiped out and at 10:00 a.m. two attacks were launched against them. One of these attacks was led by 25 tanks of the Stiffelmayer Group, the other was entrusted to 13 tanks of the 133rd Tank Regiment of the Italian Littorio Division. The Italians were driven off with the loss of four tanks and the German attack headed for 24th Armoured Brigade presenting as they did so broadside on targets to the anti-tank gunners on the Snipe at a range of 1,000 yards. Half the German tanks headed directly for the Snipe but again presented good broadside targets to the gunners of the 24th Armoured Brigade. Eight German tanks went up in flames with several others taking hits forcing the remainder to withdraw.

Cpt F.W. Marten, MC, Rifle Brigade:

> We caused a lot more casualties to the enemy, as did our tanks when they got back to hull-down positions. The crashing and noise was terrific, shells were falling all around my dug-out and each one caused an unpleasant concussion inside. I think it was conspicuous because of the two wireless aerials but we couldn't take these down without losing our communications.[19]

By 11:00 a.m. the desert was shimmering with the heat, on the Snipe men sat in their pits and trenches, sweat running down their dust caked faces. The stench was awful as the flies swarmed in black clouds upon the dead and the place was littered with blazing tanks, vehicles and carriers. Black smoke and clouds of dust thrown up by exploding shells lay like a shroud over the whole scene. However there was to be no respite for the Tommies and at 13:00 p.m. another assault was launched by Italian tanks and amid a ferocious fire fight nine Italian tanks were knocked out.

17 Letter to author from F.W. Marten 1989.
18 Ibid.
19 Ibid., F.W. Marten 1989.

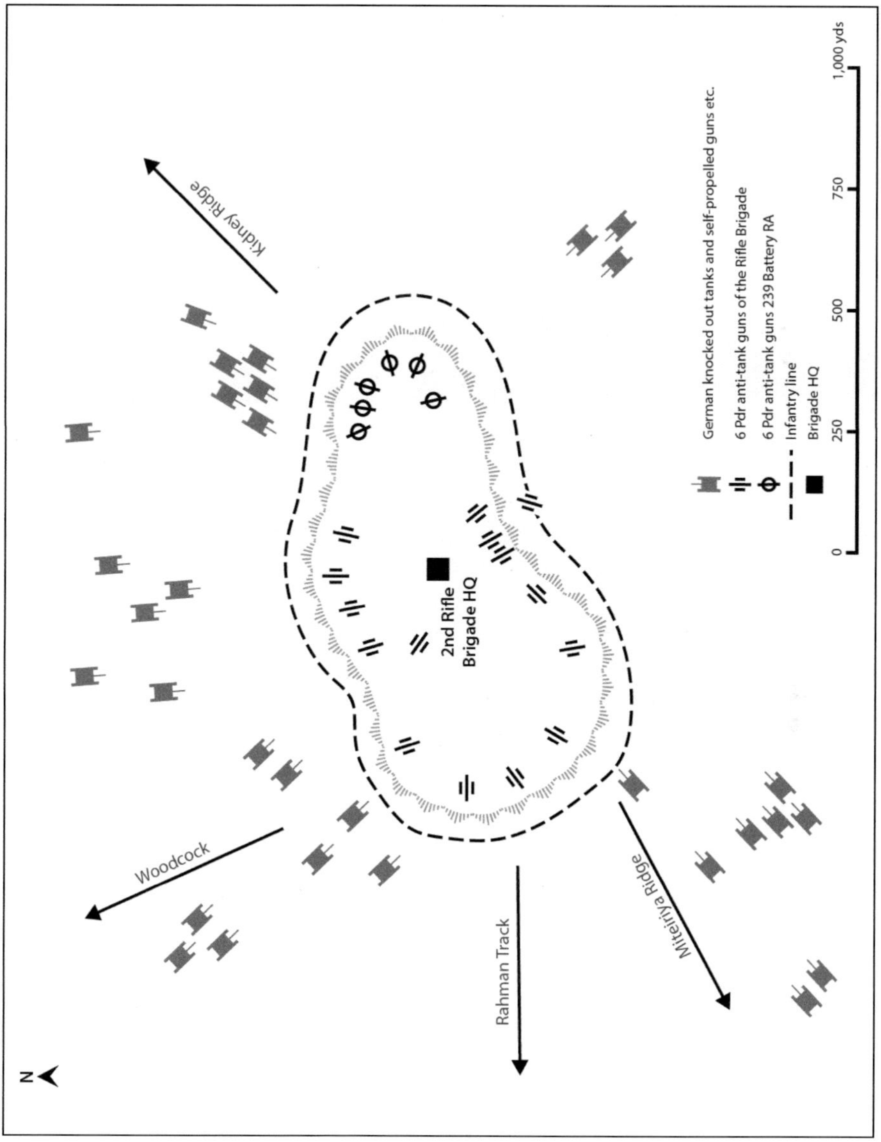

The Operation on the Snipe.

Tank tracks cover the desert as German armour deploys to the attack. (Author's collection)

Lt Colonel Vic Turner, VC, was in the part of the perimeter where the Italian attack came in at the only gun there in action, Sgt Calistan's gun. He ordered Calistan to hold his fire until the lead tank was only 600 yards away:

> Then he did some wonderful shooting, brewing up six one after the other. The remaining three tanks kept coming on blazing away with their MGs. Calistan was now almost out of ammunition so Lt Jack Toms, his platoon commander, brought up some in a jeep but the jeep was hit and set on fire about ten yards behind the gun. We managed however to man-handle the ammunition to the gun and with his next three shots Calistan scored a hat-trick, accounting for the remaining three tanks. After this he coolly turned round and said 'We haven't had a chance of brewing up this morning and as the enemy has now kindly lighted a fire for us it is a pity not to take advantage of it.' He thereupon poured some water from his water bottle into an empty tin and placed it on the burning jeep and we proceeded to have as good a cup of tea as I've ever tasted.[20]

Colonel Turner omitted in his account to mention that he was wounded in the head during this action, and Sgt Calistan recalls the moment his commanding officer was wounded:

20 D. Lee, *Up Close and Personal* (Barnsley: Frontline Books, 2015), p. 153.

> Two of my gun crew crept out into the open to get some ammo, they were under enemy fire the whole time and their progress was terribly slow. Then our platoon officer decided to reach his jeep which had four boxes of ammo on board. God knows how he got to it as they were machine-gunning the whole way. He started coming towards us when the jeep got hit and caught fire but he kept on coming. Then I had an idea, we hadn't had a thing to drink and we hadn't been able to light a fire but here was a perfectly good one. So I put a can of water on the jeep and it brewed up well enough for three cups of tea. When the next tank attack came in the colonel was acting as loader on my gun, he got a nasty wound on the head and we wanted to bind it up but he wouldn't hear of it. Keep firing, that's what he wanted and when the gun ran short of ammo he got it from the others. When the colonel was too weak to refuse attention we bound up his head and put him behind some scrub, he called out that he wanted to be kept informed of what was happening and my officer kept up a running commentary. We hit three tanks with three successive shots and the colonel yelled out 'Good work a hat-trick.' Another gun got two tanks with one shell, they were one behind the other and it passed right through the nearest one into the other and knocked out both of them.[21]

News came to the 1st Armoured Division that 21st Panzer Division had just come up from the south and were situated to the west of Kidney Ridge, the British armour would be needed to meet this new threat and the decision was taken not to support the troops on the Snipe but to leave them to their fate.

Italian tanks of the Littorio Division prepare for action. (Author's collection)

21 Ibid. p. 154.

Greater trials were still to come for the men on the Snipe as once again they were mistakenly identified as German troops by their own side and the gunners of the Royal Horse Artillery and the tanks of 2nd Armoured Brigade subjected the garrison to a heavy barrage of shell-fire at 16:00 p.m. on the 27th.

Sgt Joe Swann, DCM, noticed four lorry loads of Italian infantry with about forty men in each lorry, approaching his position. The remaining anti-tank guns were facing in the wrong direction to engage them but the bren-gunners prepared for action. He saw the commanding officer who ordered a stonk on the Italians and Sgt Swann returned to the infantry trenches:

> When I came back I lay down with a bren-gun to repel the infantry attack. The artillery opened up with shrapnel and the first shell cracked up in the air over the top of us, no casualties. The second one landed right smack on us and I was bowled over. When I picked myself up Eddie Cope was smothered in blood and my old friend Joe Flint was dead. I was walking around for about a quarter of an hour with my head ringing. After getting Cope back to first aid I went on to my other gun crew and they had sheared a bolt, they fired a couple of rounds and the main gun nut had shot off so they couldn't fire. I ordered them up to the other gun. I went forward to the infantry trench and sat down with a couple of infantry blokes. The infantry were in a trench in front of us and just below us protecting the guns. I sat there recuperating with a cup of hot water given to me by one of these chaps, it was awful. [22]

As the shelling stopped 70 German and Italian tanks and self-propelled guns could be seen forming up west of Kidney Ridge 1,200 yards away from the Snipe garrison. At 17:00 p.m. the massed enemy armour headed towards the 2nd Armoured Brigade. The British gunners on the Snipe could not believe that tanks they had been engaging all day would present their flanks to the garrison in such a careless way and so it was surmised that these units were from the newly arrived 21st Panzer Division. The phalanx of enemy tanks and guns passed the north eastern sector of the positions held by 239th Anti-tank Battery who had only four guns left that were still operational. The gunners watched this impressive spectacle moving before them in great clouds of dust but held their fire, the tanks closed with them, 500, 400, 300 yards and at 200 yards the order was given to open fire and a Mark III burst into flames with the first shots. All four guns were now scoring hits as the red hot shot drilled through the tanks armour and a dozen tanks were crippled, as the crews tried to make their escape they fell victim to the machine-gunners of the Rifle Brigade. As the sweating British gunners worked feverishly to maintain their fire heavy machine-gun fire, high

22 Manuscript sent to author by J. Swann 1991.

explosive rounds and the shrill crack of solid shot roared around and among them. This small number of anti-tank guns brought Rommel's counter attack to a halt in this sector, after 25 minutes 40 tanks were milling around in confusion with many of them burning fiercely and to make matters worse for them they were attacked by the 2nd Armoured Brigade.

German self-propelled gun. (Courtesy of H Wernamann)

A second wave of 15 Mark III tanks made a direct assault on the garrison on the Snipe, only three guns with 10 rounds of ammunition each now remained operational as the panzers came on making shrewd use of the folds in the ground. The gunners thought that this must be the end for them and watched until the tanks were nearly on top of them. At a range of only 200 yards all three guns opened fire and the effect was shattering as the four leading tanks were hit and halted, two others in the rear also burst into flames.

Cpt F.W. Marten sat in the W/T dug-out with the wounded and, plagued by flies, he watched the battle unfold:

> We were desperately short of ammunition. My dug-out contained two wounded riflemen, a wounded sapper, two signalmen, the colonel [Vic Turner, VC] who was quite delirious, Tom Bird who was out cold and quietly groaning, Charles Liddell who was very over excited, Jackie Wintour our intelligence officer in excellent and amusing form and myself. As it was a minute hole the flies were

> quite frightful, settling in hundreds on ones face and hands, the discomfort and smell was considerable. Some more of our tanks appeared about a mile and a half away and some of our own self-propelled guns gave us quite the most unpleasant quarter of an hour of an unpleasant day. The Germans started forming up for a big attack in two groups of 30 to 40 tanks, the front group past within 500 yards of our north flank. We gave them hell, setting seven on fire and stopping the attack, the second group detached fifteen tanks to attack us. They came slowly towards us head on, three got into hull-down positions behind a low ridge and from then on shelled and machine-gunned us intensively until after dark from 500 yards away. The situation was now very exciting as we had only three guns left firing on the threatened flank, none of those had more than ten rounds per gun left. They held their fire until the leading tank was only 200 yards distant and hit the first one, that gave them a shock and in the next ten minutes we set three more on fire.[23]

The remaining tanks backed away 800 yards and took a hull-down position while maintaining a galling fire with their machine-guns on the garrison. The three surviving anti-tank guns of 239th Anti-tank Battery that had repulsed this dangerous attack was left with only three rounds each, the commanders of the garrison had been so certain that their position was about to be over-run that all maps and codes had been destroyed. The scene of destruction surrounding them was staggering, over 60 burnt out tanks and self-propelled guns lay wrecked and burning before them plus numerous tracked and wheeled vehicles. The charred corpses of the crews hung out of the tank turrets or were trapped inside their machines as they burned furiously. The ground was strewn with the bodies of tank crews that had tried to escape only to be caught by the machine-gunners of the Rifle Brigade. Inside the garrisons perimeter the area was littered with the smouldering wrecks of seven British and one German tank, plus 16 carriers, several jeeps and 10 guns. The tired men of the British garrison looked out over the panorama of desolation and waited for the final attack that would envelope them, thankfully it never came

Lt Richard Flower, MC, Rifle Brigade:

> Because of all the fighting that had taken place there were dead bodied lying all around as well as the filth that lies around any battle-field. The flies were almost as bad as the enemy, they were simply appalling at Alamein and during the daytime one was pestered by literally millions of flies. Even if one had time to eat a little food and you put a bit of jam on an army biscuit, if you didn't get it in your mouth within a couple of seconds it was simply covered in flies.

23 Letter to author from F.W. Marten 1989.

> The only medical person we had there was the medical officers medical orderly, a splendid little man called Rifleman Burnthorpe. He was simply marvellous because we had a lot of casualties and despite the ground being covered with high explosive shells from the enemy and machine-gun bullets most of the time he went quietly about his job, moving from one position to another tending to the wounded. I was so delighted when I heard later he had been awarded a Military Medal for that particular action which was extremely well deserved.[24]

Survivors of the Snipe action. (Author's collection)

At 19:30 p.m. darkness fell and the enemy tanks still in hull-down positions pulled back. The British garrison commanders held a conference and made preparations to reduce their perimeter and evacuate the wounded. The Germans could be heard clearly on three sides of the Snipe as they collected their wounded and towed away any tanks that could be repaired. There was no sign of relief by 21:30 p.m. and all anti-tank guns in the area were disabled by removing the breach-blocks.

Cpt F.W. Marten watched the enemy force pull away silhouetted against the last light in the sky, the wounded were got out on the few remaining jeeps and carriers.

24 Manuscript sent to author by H. Limer 1989.

The men stood to arms expecting another attack and hoping for a relief force to come to their rescue:

> The Germans were active recovering tanks and collecting their wounded. We didn't dare to disturb them even when they came quite close, as we were still getting our wounded away. To start a fight with a superior force at this point would be a tricky business. By 22:30 p.m. no relief troops had arrived so the companies cleared off, I waited on with a few people. We hastily rendered all the guns useless, many were knocked to bits by enemy fire and others were badly damaged. I was among the last out at 23:00 p.m. with headquarters, three miles I walked and I was bloody tired. [25]

At 22:30 p.m. the British artillery began shelling the German armour in the area. The 5th Battalion Royal Sussex Regiment, 133 Brigade, 44th Home Counties Division, had been detailed to relieve the men on the Snipe but because of map reading discrepancies had gone astray and never got there.

Cpl Harold Wilmhurst, 14 Platoon, C Company, 5th Battalion Royal Sussex Regiment, recalls the confused journey and the opposition they encountered:

> We went in on 27th, on our way we passed the 51st Highlanders and they said 'you're lucky, there's nothing there now'. As we advanced all hell was let loose, we went in with bayonets fixed and shooting from the hip. The enemy machine-guns and mortars opened up and my platoon was almost wiped out. We eventually came across this anti-tank gun with Germans hiding behind it. We dealt with them by rifle and bayonet, one was wounded who begged us not to kill him. The CSM said there was a machine-gun nest on our left holding up 15 Platoon and the carrier officer came up with tools for us to dig in with, he tried to rally the troops and we saw them going in firing with brens from the hip. This officer was preparing to throw a grenade and he got shot through the shoulder. A chap called Brogden and myself patched him up as best we could with field dressings, as we finished there was a single shot and he was dead. We lay beside this huge tank that was out of action when a corporal turned up with a panzer grenadier. The corporal was wounded and he asked the CSM if he could take the prisoner out, however he couldn't do it alone so I went with this chap. I had a tommy gun that was jammed with dust and took him back to the carriers. Battalion HQ got a direct hit from a shell, two carriers were blown up and the men in them killed.

25 Manuscript sent to author by F.W. Marten 1989.

Cpl Harold Wilmhurst, 5th Battalion Royal Sussex Regiment. (Author's collection)

Slowly the survivors from the Snipe filtered back through the desert to their own lines. Major A F Flatow, 45th Battalion, Royal Tank Regiment recalls meeting some of them:

> At about 23:30 p.m. I heard the sentries challenge and I walked forward expecting to be met by a volley of shots. Some weird swaying figures approached us, they were dressed in British uniforms but I was frightened of a trick. My mind itself was full of queer tricks and I asked the first wretched man for his AB-64, he nearly cried 'Lord Sir we've been out there for twenty four hours shot at by both sides and we're all in, please take my rifle. They were it transpired the remnants of a battalion of the Rifle Brigade.[26]

The order to withdraw was given to the garrison on the Snipe and at 23:15 p.m. on 27th October the gallant but weary survivors withdrew leaving behind them a

26 Letter to author from A.F. Flatow 1991.

scene of desolation and death, this heroic action illustrated the vulnerability of tanks against well sited anti-tank guns manned by determined teams even when positioned on ground with no natural advantage. The garrison of infantry and anti-tank guns resolutely holding the Snipe had struck a heavy blow against Rommel's forces and had helped cripple the counter attack being launched, losing so many of his precious panzers was to have a detrimental effect on Rommel's future operations and would be of great help to Montgomery's future plans. Fame of their stand spread throughout Eighth Army though this success was not without cost, out of nearly 300 men that started the battle 72 had been killed or wounded along with a number of Royal Engineer casualties.

11

Preparation for Operation Supercharge

Montgomery realised that his initial thrust in the northern coastal sector had failed in its original purpose and wrote:

> The momentum of the attack [in the north], however, was diminished and X Corps had not broken out into open country. The enemy had withdrawn troops and guns from his forward positions in anticipation of our offensive, and we had therefore found him in greater depth than expected. Our break in area was still ringed by a strong ring of anti-tank guns (88s) and attempts to pierce it had been unsuccessful. By the evening of 26th October I decided to re-group in order to create fresh reserves for further offensive action.[1]

The new plan was named Operation Supercharge. Major General John Harding received orders that the 7th Armoured Division was to move their tanks from the south to the northern sector:

> I got orders to move further north to prepare for action in the northern part of the front, in reserve behind the front line where the main offensive was to take place, Operation Supercharge.[2]

Rommel took the opportunity during the lull to re-group his forces and order the 21st Panzer Division and part of the Italian Ariete Armoured Division to move from the south to the northern coastal sector with all haste, petrol supplies allowing. The diversionary attack in the south by XIII Corps had succeeded in distracting the enemy's attention by having kept the German and Italian armoured formations in the

1 B. Montgomery *Memoir* (London: Companion Book Club, 1960), p. 194.
2 C.E. Lucas-Philips *Alamein* (London: Heinemann, 1962), p. 193.

German machine-gun team at Alamein. (Author's collection)

south until 26th October. To have the greater part of Rommel's forces in the north was in theory a tactical advantage for him as it left the British more dependent on an attritional battle, but if Montgomery did not flinch from an out and out killing match it was obvious that his far greater numerical superiority would decide the issue in his favour.

While the Australians were drawing everything onto themselves the forces for the next great blow in the north were being marshalled and re-equipped by Montgomery. For Operation Supercharge he drew from formations he had held in reserve and from units that had played little direct part in the main fighting so far. The first two formations were 152nd Seaforth Brigade of the 51st Highland Division and 151st Durham Brigade of the 50th Northumbrian Division. The six battalions that made up these two brigades would have resting on their shoulders the success of the opening stages of the attack and their fighting abilities would be tested to the full. It would be the task of these two British brigades to fight their way forward into the enemy lines and create a 4,000 yard wide salient to a depth of 4,000 yards. The first objective of the infantry was 800 yards east of the Rahman Track and to the north of Tel el Aqqaqir. The most vulnerable part of the salient would be the flanks and it was expected that the enemy would attack them vigorously pouring enfilade fire into the ranks of the advancing brigades. Other infantry brigades were to be used to beat down the threats to each flank: on the left would be 133 Brigade, 44th Home Counties Division, attached to 10th Armoured Division, and on the right 28th Maori Battalion, 2nd New Zealand Division. The 8th and 50th Battalions of the Royal Tank Regiment would provide close support to the infantry and sappers that would carry out the main assault.

Troops of the Italian Bersagliere Regiment. (Author's collection)

A massive blanket of artillery fire would cover the whole operation, the guns of two armoured divisions, the 51st Highland Division, the 2nd New Zealand Division and a whole regiment from the 9th Australian Division were assembled in order to pulverise the ground before the British front line and the Axis positions beyond with shell-fire. To enable this to be done the British infantry were to be pulled back from their own front line, the first shells would be fired at 01:05a.m. just after the infantry began their advance and would continue to fall upon the British forward area until the infantry closed with it. Known enemy positions would be targeted by the gunners but most guns would lay a steady and continuous barrage over the ground the troops would be advancing over, slowly creeping forward before them. The pace of the advance would be carefully controlled, and direction would be maintained by the firing of tracer bullets over the heads of the soldiers.

The ground over which the attackers would have to cross was littered indiscriminately with fields of mines and booby traps, in between these would be well sited infantry posts equipped with machine-guns, mortars and tank turrets dug into the hard rock. To the rear of these were newly prepared gun pits that had been sited to give supporting cross-fire, the lines of anti-tank guns extended to a great depth in front of and to the rear of the Rahman Track and because most of them were new their exact location was unknown. From ground level they were almost undetectable except at close quarters.

Lt General Bernard L. Montgomery. (Author's collection)

Montgomery had reluctantly decided, because of his lack of sufficient numbers of infantry, to use his armour to attack the Rahman Track. This was to use armour as it should never be used: to attack an unbroken line of guns, the unit that would carry out this task was sure to suffer the most severe casualties. Montgomery chose the 9th Armoured Brigade for this unenviable task and the officers of its regiments were informed that if necessary 100 percent casualties were acceptable, but their objectives must be achieved.

This then was Operation Supercharge which was to be a break in by the infantry brigades, followed by a suicidal attack on an unbroken gun line by tanks, and succeeded by a thrust by the massed armoured regiments of the Eighth Army to break out into the open desert and destroy the German armour. The die was now cast, the units required to take part were informed of their roles and were ordered to gather in the northern sector.

12

Operation Supercharge 151st Brigade Moves North 2nd–4th November 1942

Meanwhile in the south a message was received at 50th Divisional Headquarters on 27th October informing the staff that a brigade would soon be required in the northern sector to join XXX Corps. On the night of the 28th 151st Brigade, 505 Field Company Royal Engineers, 149 Field Ambulance and an anti-tank battery of the Northumberland Hussars was taken out of the line. In support of the Northumbrians would be the 8th Battalion Royal Tank Regiment. All were to take part in Operation Supercharge, they were to move by night to a position in the north of the line to a concentration area behind Tel el Eisa and were relieved by the 2nd Free French Brigade.

A German half-track tows an artillery piece into position. (Author's collection)

Lt Colonel William Watson, 6th DLI, recalled the move to the north:

> On 28th October the battalion was taken out of reserve and warned for another role. At dusk, section by section, the battalion assembled and had a meal. In the early hours of 29th October we embussed in motor transport under the corps provost and moved from the southern end of the Alamein line to the northern end. The whole route was marked with lights. At three in the morning we got to an area near a railway line and by the sea. We dossed down in the soft sand and next day we all got a bathe in the sea. We were told we would come under the command of the New Zealand Division. We were told no move until tomorrow and had yet another night sleeping in the soft sand and having a bathe. But not knowing what is going to happen and what your fate is hangs heavily. It hung heavily on us all.[1]

Pte Ernest Kerens:

> It was pitch black and freezing cold when we got there, there was scores of empty slit trenches but most of them held enemy dead. We rolled two of them from a suitable one and pinched their ground sheets as they had no more use for them. Beneath these Arthur Fairclough, Ken Foster and myself tried unsuccessfully to keep warm. At 23:00 p.m. a canister of tea thickened with rum arrived. The body glowed but outside it was so much goose flesh. My thoughts started to fill with the forthcoming battle and I was scared as this was my first real battle.[2]

Lt Bill Partridge, 9th DLI:

> We trucked our way north and the moment we arrived at the concentration area the preparations for a major attack took place. We were given food and water, more than we had previously had. We could send as many air-mail cards as we wanted. All missing kit was replaced, the spare barrels of the Brens for example. The MO [Medical Officer] came round and spoke to every single man, if he judged that man was not fit to go into battle he would take him out: not for the sake of the man, but for the sake of other soldiers. He didn't take anybody out of my platoon. But every man knew that everything that could be done had been. Pride in oneself was very important, not to let the side down.

1 Manuscript sent to author by W. Ridley 1993.
2 Manuscript sent to author by E. Kerens 1991.

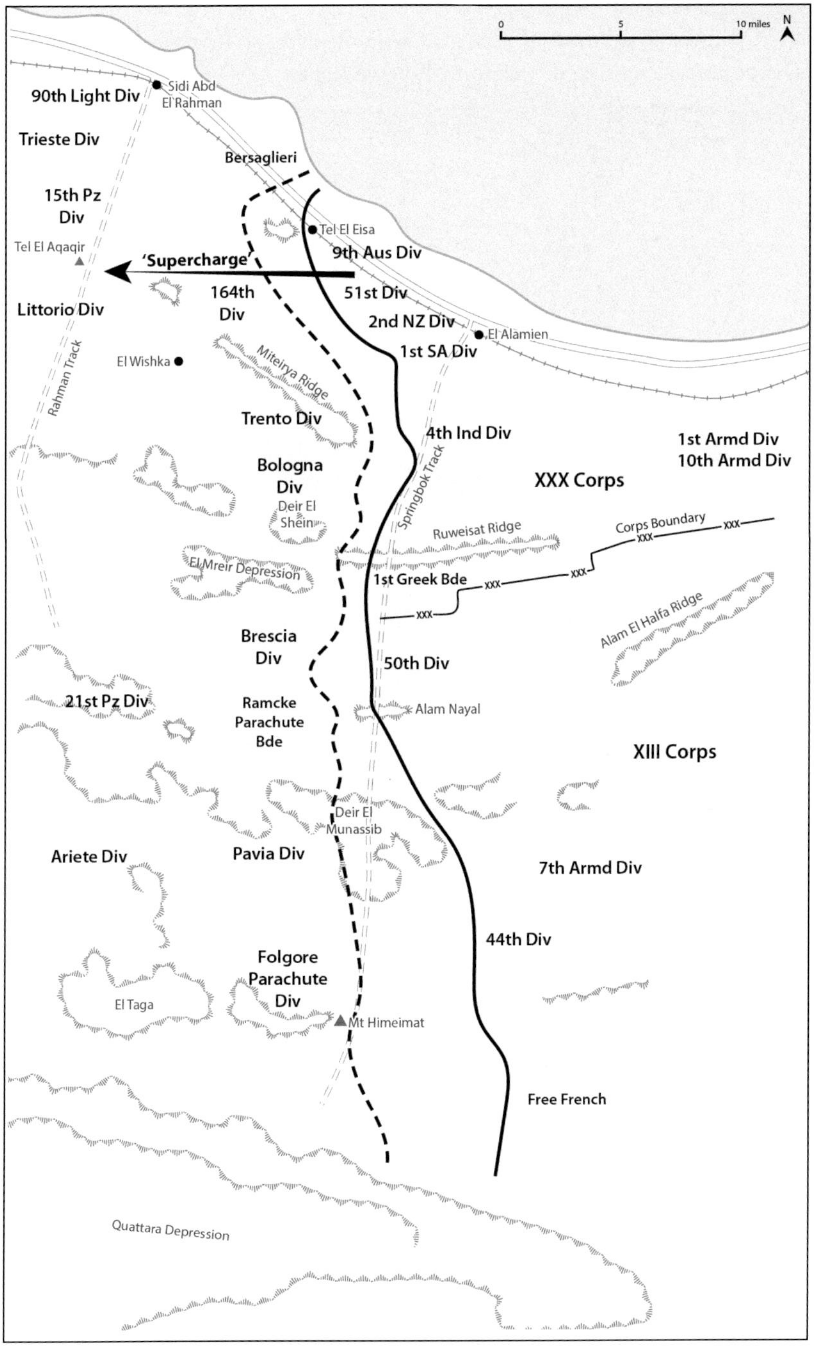

Operation Supercharge, 2nd to 4th November 1942.

When you are in a group of men you are not going to let the side down. The RSM organised zeroing of weapons then we slept.[3]

British 25 pounder crew adjust the position of their gun to meet an expected attack. (Author's collection)

Captain Peter Lewis, 8th DLI:

During the night of the 30/31st October the battalion moved in transport to an area originally held by the 51st Highland Division. It was a noisy night as we passed a lot of artillery firing in support of an Australian attack. We arrived about 03:30 a.m. in the morning. There were plenty of slit trenches already dug for us to get into. The area was packed with transport, guns, tanks and limbers. One enemy plane, only one, came over and dropped one bomb and it hit the battalion HQ office truck, which caught fire and blew up, killing Captain

3 Ibid., W. Partridge 1989.

> Julian Holgate Parker, the adjutant, who was sleeping beside the truck and not in a slit trench. The next morning a group of us, and the padre, gathered round and had a little service to bury him. It was difficult to find a little piece of desert to bury him in as the area was so packed.[4]

Captain Peter Lewis, 8th Battalion Durham Light Infantry. (Author's collection)

The Durhams arrived at their concentration area, the signs of battle were all around and it was obvious that their positions in the southern part of the line had been a rest area compared to this. The troops were hot and dusty as they settled down and it was with a feeling of relief that they learnt that the battle had been postponed for 24 hours.

Pte Ernest Kerens, 9th DLI, appreciated the kindness shown by South African troops in the area and was grateful of an extra nights' sleep:

> We were among the South African artillery, this was my trial by fire and although the guns were putting over a hell of a noisy barrage, although it was

4 J. Thompson, *Desert Victory* (London. Ebury Press, 2012]), p. 119.

Australian troops inspect a knocked out German 88mm anti-tank gun. (Author's collection)

> sheer noise, I put my head down and was soon fast asleep. We were awakened at the first cold light of dawn by an air raid on the guns, they were as common as the flies that plagued us. Among all this the South Africans had a mobile canteen and generously allowed us to use it until there was nothing left for them. The gunners shared smiles, jokes and their precious cigarettes with the Durhams, I'll never forget them. Here among the guns we spent the day and had another nights' sleep. One of our fighter planes came down nearby, I don't know if it was because the pilot was injured and didn't know what he was doing or if he just thought it was a clear stretch of sand, or if he was making sure he did not fly into our men and guns, but he made a landing in a minefield and exploded.[5]

On the morning of 1st November officers were informed by their commanders of the plan for Operation Supercharge. The 28th Maori Battalion was put under the command of 151 Brigade and it was their job to seize a strongpoint on the right flank about 500 yards from the start line. On the left of the Durhams would be the Seaforths of 152 Brigade and to their left was the infantry of 133 Brigade.

5 Manuscript sent to author by E Kerens 1991.

Lt W S (Scotty) White, 9th DLI:

> All officers were briefed by the CO, we found out this was to be the final attack, codename Supercharge. We had to break through so that the sappers could make two lanes through the minefield and get the tanks out and 'Tally Ho' into the open ground beyond. At the time he gave us the scope of the attack, the whole brigade was to take part with the 8th on our right, the 9th on the left of the 8th and the 6th in reserve to watch the right flank. On the right flank of the attack there was a Maori battalion from the New Zealand Division as additional protection for us. On our left flank we had a brigade of the 51st Highland Division. The Cheshires machine-guns would support us and there would be a massive artillery timed barrage. The idea was that, to begin with, the artillery would fire on targets 2,000 yards ahead of us, therefore we would advance and keep as close as we could to the barrage as it crept forward. Borfors guns would fire tracer to show the limits of our flanks. When the barrage was going to lift blue smoke would be fired, every detail was thought of. The attack was timed for the night of 1/2nd November, a delay of 24 hours.[6]

The stretch of desert from the start line to the Rahman Track, over which the infantry would have to march, was flat and open, rising imperceptibly over a barren stony waste. The Germans had been laying mines as fast as they could in this area, but the location of these fields was as yet unknown. The advancing British infantry would have to take their chances during the advance, which was to be a straight march, the sappers would follow behind to clear the ground for following vehicles, anti-tank units and carriers. Little detail was known about enemy positions, but air reconnaissance had shown that in addition to the infantry posts there was a line of tanks and self-propelled guns in hull down positions plus many of the dreaded 88mm guns.

On 1st November 151 Brigade joined the seemingly endless line of troops and vehicles moving forward, the sandy tracks had been churned up by thousands of tanks and vehicles. In places the fine sand was nearly a foot deep and very difficult to move through for men loaded down with rifles, bren-guns, grenades, ammunition, packs, picks and shovels. They moved to the assembly area east of Tel el Eisa Station, starting the move to the forming up position at 19:00 p.m. as the sun set. The night was lit by enemy verey lights and a bright moon, formations of RAF bombers roared overhead on their way to pound the enemy positions. The move forward was through a dusty hot landscape covered with the signs of recent battles, to their front they could hear the roar of the New Zealand artillery that got louder with each step as they approached. As the Durhams passed through the New Zealanders' positions the

6 Ibid., S. White 1994.

German troops unloading 88 ammunition. (Courtesy of Cyril Wildman)

German prisoners of war taken during Operation Supercharge. (Author's collection)

gunners were labouring, loading and firing their guns constantly, each one of them was visible as the flash from their guns lit up the night. They were firing between the coast road and the sea in support of the Australians, intended to divert the enemy's attention from the attack to come.

On the night of 1st November, as the attacking troops moved forward, 68 Wellingtons and 19 Albacores [bombers] flew over the British front heading for the enemy in perfect formation, for seven hours they repeatedly bombed positions on the Rahman Track and beyond. Six enormous explosions were heard as ammunition stores were hit and numerous large fires could be observed burning in the distance. Von Thoma's advanced Afrika Korps HQ was hit and destroyed and the ruddy glow of fires could be seen in the distance illuminating the palls of smoke that hovered over them. All of this could be seen from the British lines.

Lt Colonel William I Watson, 6th DLI:

> During the afternoon I went forward with my intelligence officer to the start line, marked out with big oil drums. The Australians had been pulled out. The intelligence officers of all battalions waited until dusk and taped out the start line and the route to it. On the way back some Stukas came over, rare birds by then, peeled off and went for some gun positions nearby. One bomb dropped close by us, my driver swung off the road and we all jumped into a ditch. An ambulance came by and stopped. The driver had all the skin flayed off his hands and arms by the shrapnel from this bomb, the chap beside him was dead and a casualty sitting in the back had been wounded again. It was a terribly near squeak for us. As we moved forward I remember passing the New Zealand gunners stripped to the waist, they were firing their guns up towards the Australian Lines as a diversion and they were just pumping the shells over. The smell was awful, dead bodies were still lying about and on the minefield wire. Then we moved into the line and just lay down.[7]

As the Durhams reached their forming up positions they lay down in an attempt to catch up on what little sleep they could. Sweating from their long approach march they now began to feel the chill of the night air as the desert cooled. A partial moon hung in the clear night sky casting a wan light as the troops waited, for two hours they dozed, chatted and checked their equipment, all anxious and all wondering if they would be among the lucky ones to come through unscathed in the coming fight.

Pte Ernest Kerens, 9th DLI, remembers the tiring march forward through sand so soft it sapped their energy:

7 H. Moses, *The Faithful Sixth* (Durham: County Durham Book, 1995), p. 252.

Italian machine-gunners of the Bersagliere Regiment. (Author's collection)

In the afternoon of 1st November the battalion began its long march to the starting point of the bridgehead attack, Supercharge. At 16:00 p.m. we halted for the evening meal, a tin of M and V, not much to die on. An hour later we continued, not so much as a column more as an untidy crocodile. Thick layers of sand clung to our skin; rags were wrapped around the rifle bolts of our weapons to ensure they would work when needed. The last few yards was through a wired off gap in the minefield, it was lined with Aussies who watched us in silence or quietly cheered us on in half whispers, 'stick em for me limey'. I got a queer feeling we were going to a dangerous sort of football match. The continuous growling of the guns and whining of the shells seemed unreal. We arrived at the starting tapes at 20:00 p.m. and we had to take cover for a while.[8]

Lt W.S. (Scotty) White, 9th DLI:

When we got to the forming up place I paired the lads up because we still had an hour or two to wait, we were in KD, summer kit, it was very cold that night

8 Manuscript sent to author by E Kerens 1991.

> and I said to the men to get together in pairs. One can sleep but take turns. At about midnight we opened the thermos flasks, each containing a gallon of cocoa and rum and thoroughly enjoyed a generous sip, it was very warming and I drank lots of it, I'd never drunk rum before. 10 minutes before zero [01:05 a.m.] we stood up, checked our equipment and fixed bayonets. The enemy was about 2,000 yards away, most men had been very quiet too, it had been a time for thought. What happens if? Everybody seemed in good heart.[9]

The sound of battle was some way off as the shivering troops waited and behind them a strange silence prevailed.

Lt Colonel William I. Watson, 6th DLI:

> There was an eerie silence, it was quite extraordinary, a deathly silence along the whole Alamein Line. Every now and then you would hear the odd shot way down south, we had an issue of rum. I should think it was badly needed and I remember the grey jars the rum was carried in being put on to the [oil] drums and I should think they are probably still there to this day. It was absolutely dead silence.[10]

A German soldier protects himself from the wind and flying sand. (Courtesy of H Wernamann)

360 field and medium guns in the British rear had swung round their muzzles until they all converged on the 4,000 yards of frontage ahead of the infantry. The gun layers were bringing the cross wires of their sights onto the lamps of their forward aiming posts and 15,000 shells stood ready to be fired during the next four and a half hours. At 00:55 a.m. the spell was broken as the artillery that was to support the attack opened up

9 J. Thompson *Desert Victory* (London: Ebury Press 2012) p. 225.

10 Letter to author W.I. Watson 1992.

from the rear with a deafeningly furious roar, shells screamed overhead exploding with earth shaking detonations before the troops and 10 minutes later the lead battalions crossed the start line on time in a veil of smoke and dust that blotted out the sky and reduced visibility to no more than 50 yards. The men of 151 Brigade moved steadily forward, German mine laying parties were found in no-man's land completely shattered mentally by the noise and violence of the barrage that had passed over them, they offered no resistance and were taken prisoner and sent to the rear.

Lt W.S. (Scotty) White, 9th DLI:

> There was a shout of 'forward' and the sound of the company commander's [Major Worral] hunting horn and the advance started. We came to the wire but had to cut it again and then we had a slight delay, the O/C had lost his hunting horn, the delay was minimal and on we went. The noise was terrific, gunfire, shell bursts, mortars, rifle fire, machine-guns, the skirl of the pipes and the shouts of our charging infantry. Above the noise of battle we could hear, from time to time, the call of our commander's hunting horn, it made us feel rather special and somehow comforted us. Now we were moving forward we no longer felt the cold, the men seemed in good heart and the adrenaline was flowing. We had not reached the actual enemy positions although we were coming across enemy slit trenches. For me these were the most exciting moments of my life to date.[11]

Captain Jim Kennedy, 9th DLI:

> I had my men in fighting patrol formation. In the centre of my own group were two men who could count paces so that they could estimate distance and not run into our own barrage. I stressed that they had to work fast to clear the area of enemy as they advanced, for the time they had till dawn was limited and by dawn they had to be in slit trenches. On my left and just five paces behind me was my batman.[12]

Pte Ernest Kerens, 9th DLI:

> Slowly we walked forward, circulation returning to frozen limbs now beginning to tingle with excitement. A single line of wire nine inches off the ground crossed our path. We checked and double checked our bearings, it could be marking a minefield. If it was it could be set for troops or tanks. This was our

11 J Thompson. *Desert Victory* (London: Ebury Press 2012) p. 238.
12 J. Sadler, *El Alamein* (Stroud: Amberley Publishing 2012), p. 202.

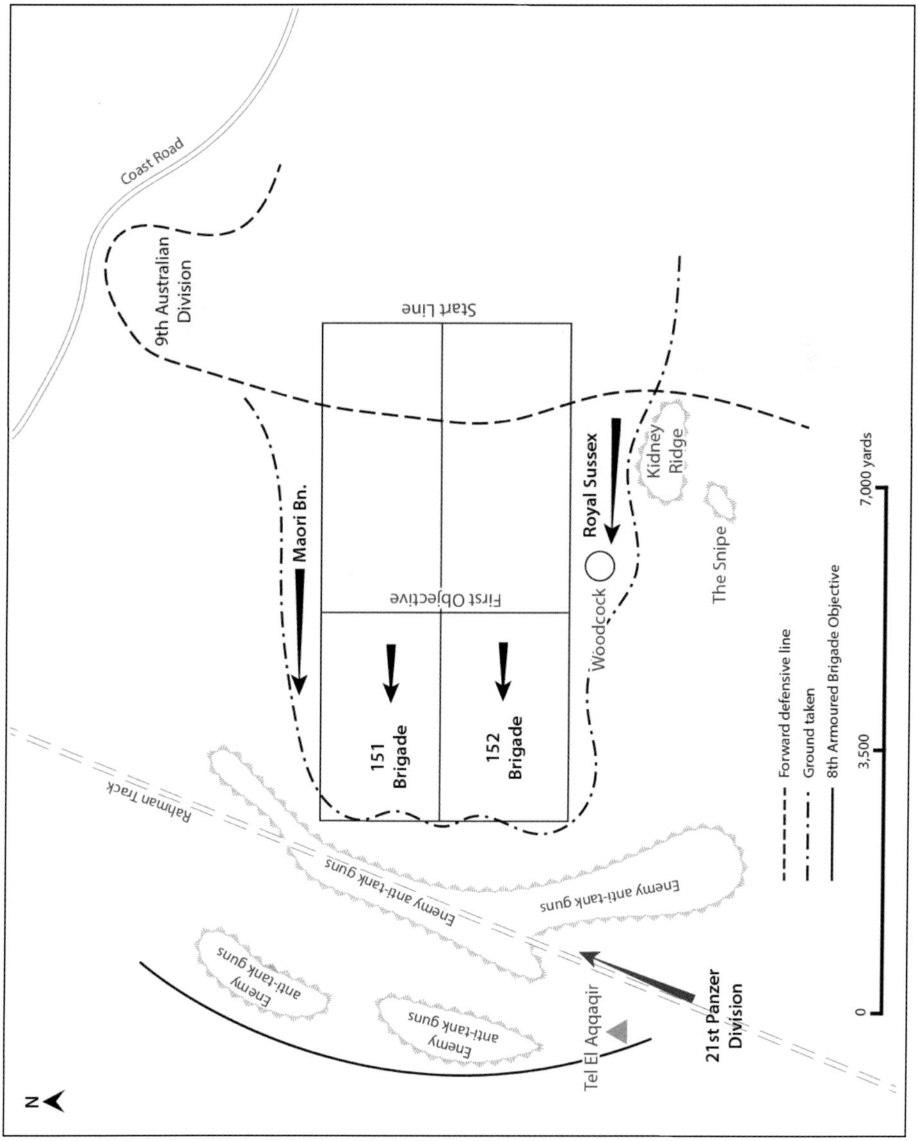

Supercharge, the battle-field.

Eighth Army troops in a forward slit trench. (Courtesy of Harry Forth)

> bearing and it had to be crossed. Our barrage from our rear was bursting to our immediate front, it was time to go. On our right a rifle fired, then another and another. The brr brr of a spandau, half a dozen of them. The barrage was literally raising the dust and through it I could see the explosions of shells and hear the rapid fire of scores and scores of spandaus and other machine-guns. My Alamein was in full swing.[13]

Pte Jackson Browne, 8th DLI:

> On the battalions flanks they had Borfors guns firing tracer every two or three minutes so that you knew the direction you were supposed to be going in, it was easy to lose direction at night in the desert. The barrage was hammering away and then they would drop a few smoke shells, they were a bloody nuisance, but when they dropped you knew the barrage was lifting and it was time for us to move on.[14]

13 Letter to author E. Kerens 1989.
14 Ibid., J Brown 1987.

Pte William Knowles was a signaller with the 8th DLI:

> We had quite some distance to walk and carried a wireless [18 set] with us, I was on the listening watch. There were three of us, I carried my pack, shovel, bren-gun magazines and bandoliers of rifle ammunition. We operated in pairs, one carried the wireless set and the other operated it. It was heavy, even on the flat ground it was a burden. The company commander was ahead of us and we were with the company main HQ in rear with the company 2I/C. It was a very flat piece of desert, firm except where it had been churned up by vehicles. There was a hell of a lot of shouting, keeping people in line and together. Every now and then we would pause and go on again. The enemy were firing machine-guns on fixed lines, you could see the tracer cutting through the darkness. We passed people lying or crouching. Then the heavier stuff started coming down and people started dropping. You couldn't stop for anyone that was wounded you knew that. A person who was hit might be lucky and be picked up by the stretcher bearers, if there was a lot of wounded the stretcher bearers couldn't cope. The wounded just lay about and any person who was badly wounded would lapse into unconsciousness. Then we had trouble with the 18 set and couldn't receive, enemy fire got stronger. I went forward to the company commander to tell him we were out of communication with battalion HQ and other companies. Things then hotted up and it was a job getting back because of the mortar and artillery fire and hoping that your own side didn't take a pot shot at you. The acrid bitter smell of cordite was very strong, later you got the smell of blood and the sweet smell of death.[15]

By 01:00 a.m. 151 and 152 Brigades were moving forward steadily following the barrage that crept before them. Machine-gun fire came from the front with mortar bombs and shells falling all around causing the first casualties. The lead battalions then came up against the enemy's main positions.

Lt Colonel William I. Watson, 6th DLI:

> In silence we walked through minefields, I had practically no casualties. Shells came screaming over our heads while Borfors Guns fired tracer over our heads to keep direction. I can remember hearing the pipers from the Highlanders on our left. The barrage thundering over your head was nerve wracking to start with, in the end it became almost a song. There were 24 [artillery] lifts before half time, very quickly the atmosphere was smoke, sand and mist. Then we saw figures with their arms up looming out of the mist, Germans and Italians

15 Interview with W. Knowles 1992.

surrendering. After we had gone about 900 yards we received enemy fire from our right which slowed us down a bit. Also we must have walked over some Italians that lay doggo as we advanced and undoubtedly one of them killed my RSM [Arthur Page, MC], the doctor tending the wounded and a sergeant who played cricket down in Dorset.[16]

German frontline positions. (Author's collection)

Captain Peter Lewis, 8th DLI:

The troops looked behind them, the whole sky was pierced with hundreds of gun flashes. Shells were screaming over us, off we went, accompanied by a crescendo of noise that was to last for three hours. There were shouted commands as we closed up to the barrage until the smoke shells were fired, which indicated that the barrage was about to lift. The smoke shells caused more confusion than they were worth. Straight away we were into the smoke and dust and muck thrown

16 H. Moses *The Faithful Sixth* (Durham: County Durham Books 1995), p. 265.

> up by the barrage. The air stank of high explosive, making the troops cough and splutter. In the distance I heard the sound of a hunting horn [this was the hunting horn of Major Teddy Worral, 9th DLI], one of the DLI company commanders in the neighbouring battalion always blew a hunting horn. German very lights went up calling for defensive fire, which came down, and some of our chaps were hit by machine-guns firing on fixed lines.[17]

Pte Jim Coglan MM, 6th DLI, was driving an ammunition lorry behind the advancing troops:

> I was advancing with the infantry when the wagon was hit and we dived off. The officer shouted 'jump, get off' we went right away from it and it burst like a fire ball. I joined the lads I'd dropped off with my rifle and we were advancing. We were getting mortared and a little small arms fire, I got wounded and dropped in with A Company, they were in slit trenches because we'd taken Gerry positions. We could see Gerry, but he was firing at us and we were firing at him. I was wounded in the back with a mortar bomb, I felt a burning feeling in the back and was knocked forward, blood was coming out of my mouth and I thought I'd had it.[18]

Pte Jim Coglan MM, 6th Battalion Durham Light Infantry. (Courtesy of John H Clark)

17 J. Thompson, *Desert Victory* (London: Ebury Press 2012), p. 251.
18 Letter to author W Ridley 1990.

The leading troops of the Durham Light Infantry stormed the first line of trenches with bayonet and bomb. German and Italian dead littered the area, many of who had been caught out in the open by the tornado of artillery shells. Some who survived were mentally shattered and almost hysterical as they were herded to the rear. It seemed impossible that anyone could have survived the barrage, but the survivors were in the main hardened veterans of the Afrika Korps who offered devoted and fierce resistance, giving nor asking for quarter.

Captain Ian English MC and bar, 8th DLI:

> In the German minefields there were mines lying about, then we came across a German lying in the open who got up and surrendered, he might have been part of a mine laying party. As we went on it was obvious that the barrage was having a tremendous effect. The Germans and Italians we came across were pretty stunned and didn't offer much resistance. We could hear the Maori battalion fighting and shouting on our right but had no idea what was happening. A German machine-gun on our right started firing tracer and this scared some of the men, but we pointed out that the rounds were going over our head.[19]

Captain Peter Lewis, 8th DLI:

> My company was hard hit and I lost my two leading platoon commanders killed. The Bofors firing tracer helped us keep direction. A Spandau opened up on our front, but he was firing high with tracer and some of our chaps ducked under the tracer and bayoneted the crew. We could see a mass of shell holes and lots of German and Italian dead. We started taking prisoners, some in a dazed and hysterical state. They wandered about and some got shot as it was sometimes difficult to tell if they were trying to surrender or making off for a slit trench. We had to keep on going behind the barrage. By now the line was probably getting a bit ragged as people paused to clear slit trenches. Some of the Germans put up quite a fight, one came out of a dugout as if he had been shot out by a launcher and came straight at me with a pistol, one of my section commanders got him with a burst from his tommy-gun. But some of them were pretty tough, they were bloody good soldiers. One bloke waited until we had got beyond him and chucked a stick grenade at us, one of my chaps went back and found him dead, he had thrown it while actually about to die.[20]

19 Ibid., I.R. English 1993.
20 Manuscript sent to author by R Hymer 1991.

A German 88 anti-tank crew in action. (Author's collection)

Opposition stiffened and visibility was down to only a few yards, dust and smoke filled the air as the opposing sides fought it out in a bitter struggle for survival. The occupants of slit trenches that had been missed fired into the backs of the rear ranks of the Durhams, these were finished off by the follow up companies. Enemy artillery fire now began to fall on the forward troops as they advanced, and casualties began to mount.

Pte Ernest Kerens, 9th DLI, was at the head of the advance:

> Bullets were now plucking at our sleeves in large numbers. The bullets and bits of shrapnel came down like a shower of deadly hailstones and we had to throw ourselves down to live. On the right a vehicle burst into flames and by the light I could see company men trying to advance. We were ahead of them but some of them were still on their feet, others were falling or had done. There were tracer bullets flying among them. Over the sounds of the barrage and small arms could be heard cursing and cries from the wounded. Someone in a pitiful voice was crying for his mother. From everywhere we heard: 'stretcher bearers, stretcher bearers!' and always the continuous noise of battle. Sight had gone but the screams and curses mixed with the chatter of the machine-guns and explosions of shells continued without pause. We hugged the ground and bullets skimmed over our heads; Ken took one in the shoulder. Suddenly Mr Henley said 'I'm going forward to see what's happening, that's all I can do'. He gave me his compass, his maps and binoculars, sent Charlie to contact the

company on the left, made some little remark and walked toward the flying tracers. That was the last Ken and I, and probably anyone else, saw of him. [Captain Raymond Wilfred Henley was killed][21]

Killed at their post: Dead German anti-tank gunners lie next to their gun. (Author's collection)

Corporal Bert Davies followed up the advanced troops in a carrier with the 6th DLI:

> The worst thing is waiting for zero hour, everybody seems to get tensed up not knowing what to expect. But once you got going you sort of lost that bad feeling in your stomach. You just followed the crowd and kept going. It was that dust as well, transport churning up the dust, choked with the dust and it was very difficult to see which was German and which were our vehicles. Many a time we ran over German trenches with Germans still in. We just jumped off the vehicle, took them out and sent them back as prisoners. They got back on their own some of them, they didn't have an escort, they'd just had enough. The noise was so great we had to shout at each other or beckon, use signs. We had instructions that if anyone was wounded he was to be left, you hadn't time because the more men who stopped to look after the wounded the less was going to the front, so if one was wounded he was looked after by the first aid lads that followed up. We heard the cries of the wounded, you wanted to go to

21 Manuscript sent to author by I.R. English 1993.

> help but orders were you weren't to go. There's got to be some sort of discipline and we knew they'd get treated alright.[22]

After a furious fight the lead companies of the Durham Brigade broke through the first German line of defence and moved into the heart of the enemy positions, passing advanced aid posts and HQ positions. They then began moving through the enemy gun lines. Commanders found it difficult to keep control of their companies and direction was hard to maintain. As each enemy post was disposed of the lead troops would increase their pace, being carried along in the euphoria of the moment. Their blood was up, and they threw themselves literally against the enemy positions. The first objective had been reached and it was in an area dotted with dug-in tanks and self-propelled guns. The lead companies waited as the barrage lingered on the first objective and when it lifted they attacked the tanks and gun positions with bayonets and grenades, killing the crews. It was then that the 6th DLI moved forward and performed a right wheel, no easy task in the dark and confusion. They now faced north to guard the brigade flank. Anti-tank guns were brought forward and the men of the 6th DLI dug in for all they were worth.

A British anti-tank gun on its portee goes into action. (Author's collection)

22 Letter to author from B. Davies 1992.

Lt Colonel William I. Watson commanded the 6th DLI:

> At the halfway line we expected to find a row of dug-in tanks. When we reached them we were to right wheel and face northwards. It was almost too good to be true when we saw them. Practically every one of the crews was still inside. I walked up to one and a corporal shouted 'I've put a sticky bomb on it', it exploded inwards and killed all of the crew, I saw A Company trying to set one tank alight. We did the right wheel and got into position and it so happened we were absolutely in the right place. Then the guns opened up again for the 8th and 9th Battalions to complete their advance to the El Rahman Track. Meanwhile we waited for dawn. Behind us the sappers were making the gap through the minefield through which we had just walked. The mines were mainly anti-tank mines, and a few may have been anti-personnel. I was fortunate we were able to walk through.[23]

Pte George Worthington MM, 6th DLI:

> The artillery and mortar fire was terrific and continuous, the ground shook beneath us and it didn't do the ears much good either. Gerry was still in his dug-outs trying to make a fight of it, most realised they were fighting a losing battle and gave themselves up. If they didn't they got killed on the spot.[24]

Pte George Worthington MM, 6th Battalion Durham Light Infantry. (Courtesy of George Worthington)

23 Manuscript to author from Mr Kilgallon 1989.
24 Interview with author George Worthington 1990.

The 8th battalion arrived at their first objective and realised that there was a great number of men who had started the attack but had not made it that far. Captain Peter Lewis took a head count:

> We came to an area of dugouts and vehicles. On our right Chris Beattie was setting fire to abandoned German tanks by firing a very light into the petrol tanks. It was still very smoky and dusty. Anything that moved or came out of the dust was usually shot and no quarter was asked or given. The battle became a series of small scale fights. At 02:30 a.m. A and B Companies arrived on the first objective; we were able to make a rough count of who was still with us as we had a pause on the first objective. Of the combined strength of A and B Companies nearly 100 men had been killed or wounded, and of the eight officers of the companies five had been killed or wounded. In A Company there was only the company commander and one platoon commander, in my company there was only me. Very soon after that I collected a gunshot wound in the right thigh while attempting to reorganise the company. I couldn't see who shot at me, you couldn't see more than 40 yards. What had been quite a busy place suddenly became deserted as the company, under the CSM and NCOs, moved off. One of my chaps put a field dressing on my wound.[25]

Captain Ian R English MC and bar, 8th DLI:

> We were now getting into the area of the German HQ, there was more enemy transport about, the moon had now risen, and it was easier to see. Out of one of these trucks a man ran away and it was light enough for me to shoot him with a rifle I was carrying, I went down on one knee and got him with my second shot. Underneath one truck there was a wounded German yelling and screaming, I asked him what he thought of Hitler now and then moved on and left him. We got more prisoners, some out of dugouts using our 36 grenades. We came across a Red Cross tent and a man came out who said in broken English he was a doctor; I ordered the troops to leave that alone and we moved on. We reached what we took to be the first objective [code name Cherry], I put up a very signal, green, red, green. We had only 15 minutes on the first objective instead of 30 as we arrived late, after a short reorganisation the smoke came down and we pushed on again.[26]

At 0:200 a.m. the lead companies of the Durham Brigade reorganised themselves and

25 Letter to author from Peter Lewis 1992.
26 Manuscript sent to author by Ian R. English 1992.

prepared to head out in the direction of the Rahman Track. At 03:00 a.m. the artillery began to fire smoke to indicate that the thundering barrage was about to lift. The weary troops struggled to their feet and advanced as close to the barrage as they could. Again the killing began as each enemy post was taken out by the infantry.

German heavy artillery battery bombards advancing British troops. (Author's collection)

Captain Ian R. English MC and bar, 8th DLI, came across a lone Italian tank:

> Presently out of the dust and smoke and general confusion, I could make out the shape of a tank. We came near and it was an Italian tank with two of the crew with their heads out of the turret. Freddie Bulmer sent two of his sections round to the right and behind it but the tank opened fire with its machine-gun and they were held up. I told Harry Welch to fire at it with a 68 [rifle] grenade, his platoon sergeant, Sergeant Martin, loaded it and fired but missed the tank by a few feet. The explosion was sufficient to frighten the tank crew, the engine

revved up and the tank turned round and went off into the night. It was a pity we had let it get away and not destroyed it. [27]

Pte Reginald Pope was with 9th DLI; he didn't think much of his chances for survival:

The first thing that comes to mind is your chances of surviving, I didn't think I would come through it, definitely not. But you take each minute, each hour, each day as it comes. During the advance I used my bayonet once or twice, that's when you come to survival, you think to yourself it's kill or be killed, it's him or me. They were hiding in trenches covered over at ground level, false ground sort of thing. When you get them in there, if you can't get at them, you chuck in a grenade and that's it. If anybody comes out you shoot them straight away no messing.[28]

Pte Reg Pope, 9th Battalion Durham Light Infantry. (Courtesy of Reg Pope)

Death in the sand. (Courtesy of Reg Pope)

27 Ibid., 1993.
28 Interview with author R. Pope 1991.

Pte Ernest Kerens, 9th DLI, searched frantically for a radio to make contact with other units:

> Almost heedless of all the bullets that whistled around I ran from one group of men to another, ran, ducked and crawled for 40 yards without finding a single officer or signal set. Nobody seemed to know or care. I found a set but both it and its signalman had been run over by a tank or something big. I came to a minefield and there was nobody in sight and no gap. It was covered with unexploded mines uncovered by the barrage, huge holes showed were many more had exploded. Over the other side of the minefield I could hear our tanks coming. A spandau was directed at me from only a few yards away, I could not see it and he had more fire power than me so I didn't bother firing back. One of our tanks also fired at me and I dived into a deep hole, each moment full of fear. Then the tank changed his target from me to the spandau. I started to crawl, picking my way through the mines towards the tanks awful carefully, until a star shell [flare] went up and then it seemed that everything was firing at me. I dived into another hole and tried to control my nerves. Every hair on my body was wet with sweat and it became very necessary to empty my bowels in a hurry. To lie on one's side while taking off my webbing and two pairs of pants was only just managed, and I did not bother to look for toilet paper. I risked another look over the top of the shell hole, brr, brr, there was plenty of that, but I did not seem to be the main target. Our tanks, on the other side of the minefield, were still a long way off. I got down in my shell hole and made a short but very sincere prayer, it had to be as I was pretty sure it would be my last. Then I stood up into the tracers and the brr, brr, and ran like hell to our tanks on the far side of the minefield. Through and over the mines I went, I may have been on them, I don't know. Over the wire and then I sheltered behind a Sherman [tank] while I got some breath back. By good luck I found myself near Nobby's carrier, I ran over and gasped 'Sir the companies are pinned down, nobody is moving, I couldn't see any officers and the adjutant has vanished'. Nobby, or rather Lt Colonel Clark, DSO, stood little more than five foot high but was five foot of solid courage, he said 'good God man show me the gap' I said 'I did not come through any gap sir', he looked at me, looked at the width of the minefield and saw how flushed and sweating I was. Then said in a thoughtful fatherly voice 'jump up and come with us son', I did not argue, I needed a fatherly voice at that moment.[29]

29 Manuscript sent to author by Ian R. English 1992.

German machine-gun team. (Author's collection)

Pte Kerens stayed in Lt Colonel Clark's carrier as he guided the first tanks through the gap in the minefield towards the advanced companies, as the tanks moved forward the carrier advanced behind them into the battle and at once the carrier came under machine-gun fire:

Pte Ernest Kerens, 9th Battalion Durham Light Infantry. (Courtesy of George Worthington)

> The carrier's bren-gunner quickly returned fire and we heard a terrified cry of 'Kamerad, Kamerad'. A huge six foot German came out of the trench with his arms in the air and shivering from head to toe. I jumped down and covered him not too keen to get close, well you never know. The carrier's bren-gunner snarled 'come here you German bastard', the poor German was scared stiff

> and still with his hands in the air started backing away. The bren-gunner let him have a full burst, the poor German, with an awful expression on his face, sank slowly flat on his face. I could have brained that bren-gunner, might have done had the C/O not been there. The same man was killed at Mareth in 1943, I wondered if there is a Valhalla for Desert Rats and if so did the two of them meet. I was sickened.[30]

Captain Ian English, MC and bar, 8th DLI, remembers the tiredness that overcame him as he reached the second objective and he ordered his men to dig-in:

Captain Ian R English, MC and Bar. 8th Battalion Durham Light Infantry. (Courtesy of Ian R English)

> Soon after we reached the second objective the barrage stopped. The silence which ensued was deathly, so great a contrast was it after the continuous noise of the last few hours. Two sensations now came over me, one was that I didn't know where anyone else was and we were alone in the desert. The second was an intense weariness after the pent-up excitement of the attack. I wanted only to lie down and sleep. This was obviously the last thing we could afford to do. After giving platoons their positions I rushed around urging men to dig as they had never dug before, we all carried a shovel, or a pick and the Durham men needed no teaching in digging. I told Busty Roberts and Lt Worley to send out contact patrols to either flank, sometime later they returned without finding anyone. L/Cpl Symonds had been unable to get through to battalion HQ so now we seemed to be out of touch with everybody and the fog of war was complete.[31]

30 Ibid. I.R. English 1992.
31 Ibid.

German heavy gun towed into position. (Author's collection)

Pte William Knowles, 8th DLI, was sent back as it was getting light through the smoke and dust with a broken radio to battalion HQ, it was found that the valves were broken, and a Royal Signals man replaced them. He then tried to make his way back to the line but found his route blocked:

> By now the tanks had moved forward, Shermans, and they were firing at the enemy in a great long line, they stopped me from getting back to the battalion. The tanks went forward a few yards, fired, then moved back and to the side, then did it again. It was a sight to see, a great arc of tanks all firing. On the flanks, about a mile away, you could just see armoured cars and light tanks shimmering in the desert. The Shermans were slowly being picked off one by one and it was a terrible thing to watch. If a tank was hit it burst into flames, I never saw anyone get out. Some shells hit the tanks and ricocheted off, you could actually see the shell twisting over and over up into the air making a peculiar noise. Then it would come down making a whirring noise, quite a lot ricocheted off like that, others just bounced off. I couldn't do anything but just sit there watching.[32]

Captain Ian R English MC and bar, 8th DLI:

32 Interview with author P. Knowles 1991.

> We began to hear the roar of tank engines and this was heartening because there were so many of them. The tanks were on our left and the leading tank was moving forward fairly slowly when 'Bang', it went up in flames, then three more. This was a ghastly sight. It was obvious there was still a screen of 88s out in front and that the tanks were silhouetted against the dawn. The Germans had marvellous targets. Within 2 or 300 yards of my company about 20 tanks were hit and not many men seemed to be getting out of the tanks. This was the 9th Armoured Brigade trying to push through.[33]

What the Durhams could not hear was only too clear to other tank crews and HQs as they listened to the transmissions of death over the air that emanated from tanks that had been hit and were burning. Fearful voices screamed out over the net crying for their mothers and loved ones as they burnt to death in some anonymous tank turret.

Lt Bill Partridge, 9th DLI, waited for the tanks on his objective and was shocked to see the carnage as they pushed through:

> It was our job to give what support we could when the tanks passed through our positions and fanned out beyond us. We were dug-in at the far end of the breach in the minefield and sited our two pounders [anti-tank guns] as the tanks came through. The men occupied shell holes or old enemy positions. We watched the ensuing tank battle and had seen tanks knocked out before, so this was nothing new. But to see it on such a scale was new to us.[34]

Captain Ian English MC and bar, 8th DLI:

> As it got lighter our guns started shelling the 88s and as an 88 is an anti-aircraft gun adapted to an anti-tank roll it is a great big gun and takes a lot of concealing. They hadn't had time to do that so were big targets. We could see the Sidi el Rahman Track about 150 yards in front of us and the mosque of the Sidi el Rahman just to our right, probably a German OP [observation post]. We saw a great big pile of sandbags concealing an 88 and fired a two inch mortar at it, which drove the crew away from the gun. As they ran we shot them and that was one less 88. The German artillery started shelling us, then a Sherman tank came up firing its Besa [machine-gun]. The tank got a tremendous crack from an 88 on our left when it was only about 20 yards from our position. Only the driver managed to stagger out and collapse on the ground. Our chaps went out and brought him in, he was terribly burned. We collected the wounded at our

33 Manuscript sent to author by I.R. English 1992.
34 Letter to author Bill Partridge 1990.

> HQ but we didn't have trenches to put them in, the poor chaps were in the open. As the day wore on the flies got terrible and the heat was a major problem for the wounded. About mid-morning 10 enemy tanks approached us and got to within 200 yards, we had no anti-tank guns as they hadn't got to us yet, so the men got their 68 grenades ready. Fortunately the tanks came no closer, but held off firing at us, but we were well dug in. The British tanks standing behind us may have put them off approaching any nearer.[35]

German 88 gun team in action. (Author's collection)

Pte John Harold Clark, 8th DLI, dug a shallow trench in the bridgehead as snipers and small arms took a steady toll of his comrades:

> During the morning we were in a very exposed and vulnerable position, it was terrifying, the 88s were pounding us and they weren't very far away either. If they didn't hit a tank their rounds would fly over us with a sharp snap as

35 Manuscript sent to author by Ian R. English 1992.

Pte John Harold Clark, 8th Battalion Durham Light Infantry. (Courtesy of John Harold Clark)

they flew to the rear. We took quite a few casualties from sniper and machine-gun fire, there was this friend of mine who was next to me, our trench gave us a bit of protection, but they got him through the head.[36]

At first light the tanks of the 8th Battalion Royal Tank Regiment and the 3rd Hussars passed through 151st Brigade's positions, Valentines, Grants and Crusaders, deploying towards the enemy. They were not popular with the infantry as they brought down enemy retaliatory shell fire which would inevitably land on them. Outlined against the dawn sky they were met with a ferocious fire from the line of 88s and anti-tank guns lined along the Rahman Track plus the fire given by enemy tanks situated further off. Many tanks were hit and burst into flames forcing both tank regiments to withdraw. Not long after the remainder of the 9th Armoured Brigade arrived with supporting arms in their rear, many of the anti-tank guns they brought with them were situated among the Durhams' positions. 151st Brigade sat tight in their trenches on November 2nd as the tank battle raged around them. Enemy fire was intense throughout the hours of daylight. The British returned this fire and overhead formations of Bostons and Baltimores [bombers] carried out hourly raids in the Rahman Track sector and beyond.

Trooper John Nichols, 8th Battalion Royal Tank Regiment, recalled the difficulties his regiment had as they moved towards the Durham's positions:

> It was like driving blindfolded through the rush hour, through the intercom our officer would shout directions, but half the time he couldn't see anything himself. Remember it was pitch dark and we were in a very thick cloud of dust. It was a real peasouper. There were frequent and annoying halts as the lane was blocked by burning vehicles, victims of the enemy bombardment. During

36 Interview with author J.H. Clark 1991.

> the advance some soft skinned vehicles and carriers belonging to the infantry [Durhams] had been hit and there were heavy casualties, but most serious to the overall grand scheme of things was the delay that such obstructions caused.[37]

Troops holding positions in the Alamein Line. (Courtesy of Brian Cook, Carnegie Heritage Centre, Hull)

Lt Colonel William I. Watson, 6th DLI, had been in action with his men for hours, they were tired and stressed and had taken many casualties. But later in the day the first cracks started to appear in the enemy troops to their front:

> The day wore on and tanks came up and tried to break through but were knocked back by the 88s. Some of them were burning in clouds of black smoke. Then all of a sudden, to our absolute joy, 90 men of the 21st Panzer Grenadier Regiment, including their C/O, the equivalent of a brigadier, put up their hands. It was a wonderful sight, a row of German soldiers standing up out of their sangars and holes in the ground, putting their hands up and marching in. Jimmy Chapman, one of my company commanders, brought them in. I went

37 Letter to author John Nichols 1993.

> over, their C/O was a great big man, a typical Prussian, he had his greatcoat on. I asked him what his regiment was, he asked if I spoke German and I said no. He apologised for the dirty state his men were in and said that some of them were badly wounded. I put the C/O and the wounded on carriers and sent them to brigade HQ. This bucked us up no end but the 88s were still being a nuisance.[38]

The strain of battle was now starting to show on most men, some worse than others and men showed great compassion for each other in these trying circumstances. Pte William Knowles, 8th DLI, was in a truck that had been brought to the forward area, he and his comrades got permission from CSM Branagan to brew up in a captured bunker:

> We came across a huge bunker and made straight for it, it had contained a big German mobile gun, the CSM seemed to know about it. We stopped the truck and as we were getting off a Breda [Italian machine-gun] opened up, it had a distinctive sound and bullets whizzed over us, it fired a heavier bullet than the 303 our machine-guns used. We went down into the bunker and somebody said, 'I could do with a cup of tea' so Branagan said 'why not, let's all have a cup of tea'. We had to find something to boil water in and could use petrol and sand to make a fire. In the corner was a very clean huge round tin, biggest tin I've ever seen about a foot across. We cleaned it out, could have been a pee can. We had some hard tack and bully beef and about half a cup of tea which fortified us. Looking out of the corner of my eye I saw the driver who I thought was asleep, a big ginger haired bloke, he didn't have any tea. The batman was about to open his mouth and go across and speak to the driver but Branagan grabbed him before he got a word out and held his finger up to his mouth, glaring at me as he did the same. I looked at this bloke sitting in the corner, he was far away, his eyes were open, red and glaring, sitting all tense. Branagan was well known in the battalion as a tartar. He was a devil for discipline, everything had to be just so for him. I thought what a humane person this hard man really was, he wasn't going to let anyone worry the driver.[39]

Pte William Knowles, 8th DLI, was given instructions to go back and collect a truck and to bring it forward through the minefield gap. On his way he came across troops panicking in fear of a counter-attack:

38 Manuscript sent to author by Ian R. English 1992.
39 Manuscript sent to author by John Harold Clark 1994.

German tank in a hull-down defensive position. (Author's collection)

> Some prisoners started trickling back through our sector and as I approached the gap I saw some troops, not Durhams, I don't know who they were, and they were milling about over a wide area. Away on the flank there were some light armoured vehicles, some of these troops started yelling at the tops of their voices, panic stricken, 'they're counter-attacking, they're counter-attacking', I thought no they are not, not with tanks in front of us. I thought this was a load of rubbish, but there was a blind panic among these people milling around the gap. I noticed that these light vehicles on the flanks had kicked up a lot of dust, I though they wouldn't be beetling back like that in a counter-attack, more likely they were coming back to re-fuel and get fixed up. I got to the edge of the gap and there was a little tent on the other side. Out strode this officer with all his rank badges on his shoulders immaculately dressed, his cap had a red band. He used every expletive in the world as he shouted at these soldiers 'you bloody cowards, get out of here, there is no bloody counter-attack'. This bloke stalks into the middle of this mob and the panic stopped, they drifted off. By now the battalion was on its final objective.[40]

40 Ibid., W. Knowles 1994.

The wounded were now being taken to the rear as ambulances arrived to load them up. Lt Scotty White, 9th DLI, was helping gather the wounded near him though he had been hit himself:

> By heaving and hauling we got the other wounded to my little piece of raised ground so I could keep an eye on them. As the stretcher bearers went off the meat wagon [ambulance] came up. I was very angry, thinking 'three years of doing nothing, just training, and then this happens'. It was that sort of feeling; I wasn't concerned about the wound. We were taken off to the RAP [Regimental Aid Post] and from there to a place where we could be given treatment for our wounds, including surgery. I'm not sure how far back this was, it seemed to me to be not far behind our start line. Here we lay on stretchers. The C/O of the Maori battalion was there in a dreadful state with a bullet wound in the mouth, his jaw was broken, and blood was everywhere. He was stripped to the waist and was magnificent, I thought what a waste. They took my pistol off me, all the ammunition and grenades, by now I was beginning to feel my wound. They don't tell you anything except you'll be alright lad. A South African female nurse lifted me up onto the operating stretcher, lovely girl, built like a tank.[41]

Other wounded men missed the transport to the rear and needed to be carried in if they were to get away from the fighting that was still going on around them. Captain Peter Lewis, 8th DLI, couldn't walk and shouted to a group of British soldiers that were escorting prisoners into captivity:

> The only way they could get me back was for four Germans to carry me on their shoulders. I was hoisted onto these shoulders and was higher than I wanted to be as stray bullets were still flying about and I felt vulnerable. It was a remarkable two mile journey. The crash of bursting shells grew fainter and fainter as the barrage moved away and we walked in the opposite direction. There was no one else in sight and we might have been walking on the moon. As we reached the British Lines from where we had started we saw our tanks moving forward. I eventually got back to 50th Division's field ambulance. I lay next a young Italian officer who asked me for a cigarette, turned away and died.[42]

As the morning wore on the bombing RAF formations were pummelling the German positions at regular intervals, it was not long before cracks began to show in the

41 Ibid., Reg Pope 1990.
42 Manuscript sent to Author by Ian R. English 1990.

Wounded men of the Durham Brigade. (Courtesy of William Ridley)

German units opposite the Durhams. Captain Ian R English, 8th DLI, MC and bar remembers:

> After about three or four hours of being bombarded very accurately by the air force lots of Germans got up and walked across the desert and gave themselves up. Things were improving and the company was in good spirits again after the terrible tank losses. Our gunners were shooting well, and we were doing alright. I reckoned we had lost about 20 men. There was a bit of a diversion when an 88, towed by a half-track, drove across our front. Everybody fired at it, but it kept going. Eventually a shell hit the half-track so that the gun wasn't going anywhere. The men had been carrying a packet of biscuits and a tin of bully each, so we weren't going hungry. But we were a bit short of ammunition, particularly grenades. Shortly after mid-day Private Davis arrived back having had a scary trek from battalion HQ with the message that C Company was to withdraw and to confirm to 9th and 6th DLI. I thought we were well situated, and this withdrawal worried me as we had to go over open desert. I ordered 14 Platoon to go first followed by 13 and 15 Platoons in open order, leaving their bren-guns to go last. I ordered 13 Platoon Commander, Harry Welsh, to take

charge of the operation and tell the C/O that it was imperative to get transport forward to evacuate the wounded. I decided to stay with the wounded and Private Crawley stayed with me. I counted the company and there were 50 to 60 men, so we had lost about 35. The withdrawal went off well, there was a bit of shelling but no casualties. Crawley and I had what seemed to be an interminable wait, but about an hour and a half later a carrier flying the Red Cross flag and a jeep came up. We loaded the men on to these vehicles and while we were doing this we were bombed by Stukas which didn't improve things. In fact it was a lot of dust and noise, but the wounded lying there were scared stiff and so were we. We got back to battalion HQ and I was shown my new area where the men were already well dug-in and I learned about our casualties, including my 2nd I/C Ian Turnbull, whom no one had seen since crossing the start line. He was reported missing. but no one had seen him wounded, he disappeared off the face of the earth.

Captain I.S. Turnbull was killed in action on 2nd November 1942.[43]

German prisoners marching into captivity. (Courtesy of John Harold Clark)

43 Ibid., I.R. English 1993.

The tank of Trooper John Nichols, 8th Battalion Royal Tank Regiment, headed for the German gun line on the Rahman Track, he had been through this kind of thing before and felt no excitement in the attack:

> After a certain amount of time you look around the faces of your mates and realise with a shock how few of the original mob are left. Then you know it's only a matter of time before you get yours. All I wanted to do was to get across that bloody ground and through the guns. As I passed one [German] gun position the gunners were prostrate with fear, I saw that the gun couldn't be swung round very easily, they were only good for action in front. So once we passed them they couldn't really shoot us up the arse. We were hit four times, but nothing penetrated, and we got underway. I felt sorry for the ammo truck drivers and those driving the petrol lorries. They had come through the same shit we did but in unarmoured vehicles and their cargo was lethal, one hit and it was curtains. Just to the right of our machine there must have been an 88 or something very heavy. Bang, bang, bang just like that and a whole troop went up in flames. In fact the whole ground ahead of us was full of burning tanks and we knew we were next. I saw one Cruiser tank fire at a Gerry gun without effect, and I could well imagine the commander's fury at having such a stupid weapon. He just swung the tank round and ran over the gun pit, the gun stuck up in the air and the tank was out, I didn't see anybody get out of the tank or the gun pit. Even in daylight you couldn't see the guns until they fired at you, if they missed you had to get them with your first shot or you were dead. There was no mercy shown to crews, tank crews or gun crews, we shot them as they ran, and they did the same to us when we bailed out. It wasn't such a gentleman's war as a lot of people like to make out it was.[44]

The German anti-tank screen on and beyond the Rahman Track continued to take a heavy toll of the British armour that had survived the charge, the British survivors looked on as German panzer regiments, under the protective fire of their 88s, move slowly towards them and the British units that had been so badly mauled turned to face them with their much lighter armaments. Of the 94 British tanks that had pressed on through the infantry positions 75 were left behind as burning wrecks and casualties among the crews were more than 50 percent. The tanks that remained waited anxiously for the rest of their comrades to arrive.

By 4th November the 7th and 10th Armoured Divisions were streaming out into open country, Rommel's losses were so heavy he felt obliged to withdraw that night, but Hitler forced him to hold on. The confusion in the German ranks was added to

44 Interview with author John Nichols 1989.

German officers examine a captured British tank. (Author's collection)

as order and counter order was issued. That night the 51st Highland Division and 4th Indian Division attacked and smashed through the deadlock.

Alfons Selmayr, 5th Panzer Regiment, 15th Panzer Division, listened to the radio traffic and knew that the end was near:

> Shot up panzers lay all around, Tommy stayed outside range but with his wide reaching and superior guns he bested us convincingly. The Sherman tanks were proving their worth and for the first time we noticed the enemy's material superiority. The new M4 was the equal of the long barrelled Mark 1V and superior to the Mark 111. In the south I could see huge smoke and dust clouds, everywhere was burning. We were down to only 30 panzers against a good 300, we urgently requested support from Panzer Regiment 8. Instead we were ordered to counter-attack across a table top flat approach against Tommy, who was not only superior in numbers but also in armour and guns. I overheard the radio exchanges between the commander of the regiment, Hauptmann von Senfft, and our battalion commander, Oberleutnant Mildebrath, who was ordered to attack, he responded: 'an attack is nonsense', Senfft agreed 'correct but orders are orders'. We hung back as the first panzers burst into flames

after travelling only 100 metres. The Italians fared no better, despite their light armour they drove forward with magnificent daring and were of course heart-rendingly shot to pieces.[45]

Blazing tanks and vehicles on the battlefield. (Author's collection)

The progress of the Durham Brigade during Operation Supercharge was harsh and bloody, but despite this they reached their final objective with minutes to spare. By four in the morning of the 3rd November, as the dust of the barrage settled and a partial moon threw a faint light over the scene, they were digging into the hard rocky ground. From the rear the New Zealand sappers came up and began clearing mines and obstacles to make a safe path for the armour to pass through. By 05:00 a.m. the fighting vehicles of the 6th DLI had moved up led by Maurice Kirby and soon afterwards ambulances crammed with wounded were heading for the casualty clearing stations in the rear. During the latter stages of the fighting communications had been lost for a while with the forward units and it was not until 05:30 a.m. that General Freyberg informed XXX Corps that the new front was stable. The Maoris also had a

45 Manuscript sent to author by H. Wernamann 1987.

fierce fight to obtain their limited objective, which was Point 29, a strongpoint on the Durhams' right flank. They took 100 casualties and their C/O, Fred Baker, had his tongue torn out by a bullet.

Battlefield graves of an English and Scottish soldier. (Courtesy of Ian R English)

On the left flank the Seaforth Brigade captured all of their objectives, their attack came up against dug-in tanks and as they consolidated their new positions the enemy armour was all around them. Their communications were good and when they were threatened they could call down artillery support that arrived promptly and on target. Casualties had not been severe during the advance but once on their objectives heavy and continuous artillery fire pounded their positions. In the succeeding hours the 5th Seaforths lost 12 officers and 150 men. On the extreme left flank the Sussex Brigade captured the strong point code named Woodcock.

Although the new positions held by the Durhams on the northern extremity was somewhat tenuous Freyberg regarded the night's work by the Scots and Durham infantry, the sappers and the artillery support from X and XXX Corps as an outstanding success. Not only had a gap been formed to funnel the armour through, but severe casualties had been inflicted on the Axis Forces in this battle of attrition. The attacking

British battalions had been led to believe that the enemy was not as thick on the ground as they found out they were and they had been overcome in a battle fought in the old fashioned First World War way.

The Brigades that had taken part in Operation Supercharge received news of their relief as darkness fell, firing ceased and the fierce glow of burning tanks around the battle area slowly died down. In the distance the sound of moving enemy transports could be heard. These momentous events in the north had an effect in the south, XIII Corps was left with only two divisions, 44th Home Counties Division and 50th Northumbrian Division, the latter consisting of 69 Brigade, 1st Greek Brigade and 2nd Free French Brigade. The Frenchmen relieved 69 Brigade who took over positions on Ruweisat Ridge from the 4th Indian Division.

Battlefield graves of a German tank crew in front of their knocked-out Panzer. (Author's collection)

In the south XIII Corps significantly reported the quiet but steady thinning out of enemy troops from the forward areas, the Desert Air Force reported an increasing volume of movement along the coast road westward as well as movements to the enemy rear along the numerous desert tracks. In the north the Australians sent out patrols seeking information on the enemy dispositions and in the south 50th Northumbrian Division and 44th Home Counties Division did the same. Montgomery had no wish to see his opponents make a general withdrawal as he wanted them to fight it out where they stood thus ensuring their total destruction. By remaining in their present positions for so long he had been able to give them such a severe battering that the end could not be far away. However all the reports that were flooding in gave Montgomery a clear indication that the enemy was on the brink of a general withdrawal. Montgomery correctly surmised that Rommel would try to make a stand on the coastal escarpment at Fuka but wanted to cut him off before he got there. He now made plans for a swift follow-up operation on the evening of the 3rd November which capitalised on the successful minor attacks on the positions known as the Snipe and Skinflint made the night before. After a corridor had been made south of Tel el Aqqaqir the 7th Armoured Division and the New Zealanders would be launched and would sweep out into open country. Both would then wheel right to the coast and cut off the Afrika Korps line of retreat. Montgomery's three pronged attack on 4th November would be made by 153 Brigade and 154 Brigade, supported by 8th Battalion Royal Tank Regiment, and 5th Indian Brigade, 4th Indian Division, supported by 50th Battalion Royal Tank Regiment.

An 88 anti-tank gun in action. The empty shell case has just been expelled to the left of the picture. (Author's collection)

The weary troops and commanders of the Eighth Army were by now battle weary, men were strained and irritable, General Wimberley, CO 51st Highland Division, was informed by his superiors that the objective of the Gordons on the Rahman Track was now in the possession of the 8th Armoured Brigade and that all they had to do was to occupy it. The air and artillery support planned was accordingly cancelled, Wimberley said this was not born out by the reports he had received and duly asked for a barrage to be provided, his request was denied but a smoke screen would be provided to guide the troops onto their objective. The Gordons began their approach march from the Skinflint position mounted on the Valentine tanks of 8th RTR. As they moved forward they came under heavy enemy fire and were brought to an abrupt halt. Supporting artillery fire was called for but radio links failed, the troops halted and dug-in to get some protection.

Collecting the dead. (Courtesy of Norman Hardy)

The attacking formations suffered nearly 100 casualties and 20 Valentines were hit or destroyed. Wimberley was at the end of his tether as he watched tanks returning loaded up with dead Scotsmen, in his journal he wrote:

> Never again, so many attacks, so many switches of troops. As soon as one show is over we begin preparing for the next.

The other two prongs of the attack were hard fought but successful, the breakout had been established and the hunt was on. In the south the divisions of XIII Corps prepared to follow up the now demoralised Italian units, they had little food or supplies, and

German prisoners being marched into captivity. (Courtesy of Wilf Gilson)

German gunners hitch up their gun to its transport as they prepare to retreat. (Courtesy of H Wernamann)

Rommel had taken their transport for his German forces, he had in effect abandoned them to their fate. Wimberley recorded:

> All very exhilarating in spite of fatigue. Bodies of dispirited prisoners crocodiling in and our armour pouring forward. On every hand lay the wreckage and the flotsam, human and material, of a broken army. This was victory at last. This was conclusive, undeniable, irreversible victory.

It is said by some that the battle of El Alamein ended at dawn on 4th November 1942, as the Axis Forces broke away with the British in hot pursuit. However there was still a great deal of fighting to be done, Alamein was just a beginning and not an end, it did not end the war in Africa but set in motion a series of events that resulted in an allied victory on that continent. Who knew at the time where the axis retreat would end? Land battles of increasing ferocity would be fought in the coming weeks, but the Axis Forces would never again regain the military initiative. Alamein was to be the first in a line of victories that gave hope to the people of Britain.

Burying the British dead at Alamein. (Author's collection)

Lt R J Jeffery, Carrier Battalion, 44th Reconnaissance Regiment, should have the last word as he looks back on his time with the renowned Eighth Army:

> My memory still sees vividly the desert panorama, the trig points [piles of cans], the joyous scene when the water cart, mail or canteen arrived. Yet again the little desert rat [the jerboa], the wandering Arabs, the raiding Messerschmitt and not least the desert storms. A rain shower would make the desert suddenly become full of naked soldiers primitively and sensuously indulging in the soft cooling sweetness of the rain. And afterwards the Desert Rose bloomed for a day. There followed the agony of friends killed or badly wounded and the inner thoughts of inadequacy as the war lords wheeled their chariots inexorably on. To have survived makes one proud to have been a part of such a magnificent army and humble in the knowledge that one has been spared.[46]

46 R.J. Jeffery letter 1989.

Appendix A

Eighth Army Order of Battle October – November 1942

XXX Corps.
Lt General Oliver Leese

4th Indian Division
Major General F.I.S. Tucker
5th Indian Brigade, 7th Indian Brigade, 161st Indian Brigade

51st Highland Division
Major General D.N. Wimberley.
152nd Brigade, 153 Brigade, 154th Brigade

9th Australian Division.
Major General L.J. Morshead
20th Australian Brigade, 24th Australian Brigade, 26th Australian Brigade

2nd New Zealand Division.
Major General B.C. Freyberg.
5th New Zealand Brigade, 6th New Zealand Brigade,
9th Armoured Brigade (attached)

1st South African Division
Major General D.H. Pienaar
1st South African Brigade, 2nd South African Brigade
3rd South African Brigade.

23rd Armoured Brigade Group.
Brigadier General G.W. Richards.

X Corps.
Lt General H. Lumsden.

1st Armoured Division
Major General R. Briggs
2nd Armoured Brigade, 7th Motor Brigade

10th Armoured Division
Major General A.H. Gatehouse.
8th Armoured Brigade, 24th Armoured Brigade, 133rd Lorried Infantry Brigade.

XIII Corps
Lt General B.G. Horrocks

50th Northumbrian Division
Major General J.S. Nichols
69th Brigade, 151st Brigade, 1st Greek Brigade

44th Home Counties Division
Major General I.T.P. Hughes
131st Brigade, 132nd Brigade.

2nd Free French Brigade.
General M.P. Koenig

7th Armoured Division.
Major General A.F. Harding
4th Light Armoured Brigade, 22nd Armoured Brigade, 131st Infantry Brigade

Appendix B

DAK/Afrika Korps Order of Battle October – November 1942

Panzergruppe Afrika
General G. Stumme

221st medium and heavy batteries, 612th Anti-aircraft Battalions,
19th Anti-aircraft division.

Afrika Korps
Lt General W.R. von Thoma

15th Panzer Division
Major General G. von Vaerst.
8th Tank Regiment. 113th Panzer Grenadier Regiment, 33rd Artillery Regiment, 33rd Anti-tank Battalion, 33rd Engineer Battalion

21st Panzer Division
Major General H. von Randow
5th Tank Battalion, 104th Panzer Grenadier Regiment, 155th Artillery Regiment, 39th Anti-tank Battalion, 200th Engineer Battalion

90th Light Division
Major General T.G. von Sponeck
155th Panzer Grenadier Regiment, 200th Panzer Grenadier Regiment,
346th Panzer Grenadier Regiment, 190th Artillery Regiment,
190th Anti-tank Battalion, 605th Anti-tank Battalion,
109th Anti-aircraft Battalion, 606th Anti-aircraft Battalion

164th Light Division
Major General C.H. Lungershausen

125th Infantry Regiment, 382nd Infantry Regiment, 433rd In Infantry Regiment. 220th Artillery Regiment, 220th Engineer Battalion, 220th Cyclist Unit, 609th Anti-aircraft Battalion

Reconnaissance Gruppe HQ

15th Lorried Infantry Brigade

3rd, 33rd and 508th Reconnaissance Units

Ramcke Parachute Brigade
Major General B. Ramcke
Three battalions of 2nd, 3rd and Lehrbatallion Burckhardt,
Parachute Battery, Parachute Anti-tank Battalion

Appendix C

Italian Army Order of Battle October – November 1942

X Corps
Lt General E. Nebba

Brescia Division
Major General B. Brunetti
19th Infantry Regiment, 20th Infantry Regiment, 1st Mobile Artillery Regiment, 27th Engineer Regiment

Folgore Parachute Division
Major General E. Frattini

185th, 186th and 187th Infantry Regiments

1st and 2nd Battalions, Anti-tank Regiment
VIII Demolition Engineer Battalion

Pavia Division
Brigadier General N. Scattaglia
27th and 28th Infantry Regiments, 26th Artillery Regiment, 17th Engineer Battalion, 9th Bersagliere Regiment, 16th Corps Artillery Group

XX Corps.
Lt General G. de Stephanis

Ariete Armoured Division
Brigadier General F. Arena
132nd Tank Regiment, 8th Bersagliere Regiment, 132nd Artillery Regiment, 3rd Armoured Cavalry Group, 132nd Engineer Battalion

Littorio Armoured Division
Major General G. Bitossi
133rd Tank Regiment, 12th Bersagliere Regiment, 3rd Armoured Cavalry Group, 3rd and 133rd Artillery Regiments

Trieste Motorised Division.
Brigadier General F. La Ferla

11th Tank Battalion, 65th and 6th Infantry Regiments, 21st Artillery Regiment, 8th Armoured Bersagliere Regiment, 52nd Engineer Battalion

XXI Corps
Lt General E. Navarini

Trento Division
Brigadier General G. Masina
61st Infantry Regiment, 62nd Infantry Regiment, 46th Artillery Regiment

Bologna Division
Major General A. Gloria
39th Infantry Regiment, 40th Infantry Regiment, 205th Artillery Regiment, 25th Engineer Battalion, 7th Bersagliere Regiment, 24th Corps Artillery Group, 8th Army Artillery Group

Army Reserve
35th Infantry Regiment, 36th Infantry Regiment
3rd Motorised Artillery Regiment, Two Battalions of Young Fascist Division

Appendix D

7th Armoured Division Order of Battle October – November 1942

4th Light Armoured Brigade
4th/8th Hussars, 2nd Scots Greys, 3rd Regiment Royal Horse Artillery,
One troop from 42nd Battery, 15th Light Anti-aircraft Regiment,
One troop from 21st Field Squadron, Royal Engineers,
5th and 58th Support Coys, Royal Army service Corps,
14th Light Field Ambulance, Royal Army Medical Corps.

22nd Armoured Brigade
1st and 5th Battalions Royal Tank Regiment, 4th County of London Yeomanry, 1st Battalion the Rifle Brigade,
131st Infantry Brigade, 5th, 6th and 7th Queen's Regiment,
11th Hussars, 7th Division Signals, 1st Household Cavalry,
44th Reconnaissance Regiment, 2nd Derbyshire Yeomanry

Royal Artillery.
4th Field Regiment, 97th (Kent Yeomanry) Field Regiment.
65th (Suffolk and Norfolk) Anti-tank Regiment,
15th (Isle of Man) Light Anti-aircraft Regiment

Royal Engineers
4th and 21st Field Squadrons, 143rd Field Park Squadron

Royal Army Medical Corps
2nd Light Field Ambulance

2nd Free French Brigade

General Marie Pierre Koenig.

5th and 11th Battalions de Marche
21st and 23rd North African Anti-tank Companies,
2nd Company Free French Engineers

Appendix E

2nd New Zealand Division Order of Battle Operation Supercharge, 2nd November 1942

9th Armoured Brigade.
3rd Hussars, Royal Wiltshire Yeomanry, 14th Sherwood Foresters, 31st New Zealand Anti-tank Battery

23rd Armoured Brigade
8th, 46th and 50th Battalions Royal Tank Regiment,
121st Field Regiment, Royal Artillery,
168th Light Anti-aircraft Regiment, Royal Artillery

2nd New Zealand Division Cavalry

New Zealand Artillery.
4th, 5th and 6th Field Regiments,
7th Anti-tank Regiment. 14th Light Anti-aircraft Regiment
New Zealand Engineers,
6th, 7th and 8th Field Companies. 5th Field Park Company,

One Field Company of 51st Highland Division

2nd New Zealand Division Signals

151st Infantry Brigade
6th, 8th and 9th Battalions Durham Light Infantry
34th New Zealand Anti-tank Battery. 30 Corps Anti-tank Battery,

Two companies of the 27th New Zealand Machine-gun Battalion

152nd Infantry Brigade
2nd and 5th Battalions Seaforth Highlanders,
5th Battalion Cameron Highlanders,
One Machine-gun Company of 7th Middlesex Regiment,
One battery from the 61st Anti-tank Regiment, Royal Artillery

5th New Zealand Infantry Brigade
21st, 22nd and 23rd New Zealand Battalions,
28th Maori Battalion. 32nd Anti-tank Battery,
One company of 27th New Zealand Machine-gun Battalion
6th New Zealand Infantry Brigade.
24th, 25th and 26th New Zealand Battalions, 33rd Anti-tank Battery.
One company of 27th New Zealand Machine-gun Battalion.

Appendix F

44th Home Counties Division Order of Battle October 1942

Commander Major General I.T.P. Hughes.
131st Infantry Brigade.
Officer Commanding Brigadier W.D. Stamer

5th, 6th and 7th Battalions Queen's Royal West Surrey Regiment

Attached to 7th Armoured Division.

132nd Infantry Brigade
Brigadier L. Whistler.

2nd Battalion Royal East Kent Regiment

4th and 5th Battalions Royal West Kent Regiment.

133rd Infantry Brigade.
Brigadier A.W. Lee.

2nd, 4th and 5th Battalions Royal Sussex Regiment.

Attached to 8th Armoured Division 8th September 1942;
to 10th Armoured Division 29th September 1942.

Appendix G

50th Northumbrian Division Order of Battle October – November 1942

69th Infantry Brigade

Commander Brigadier E.C. Cooke-Collis DSO

5th Battalion East Yorkshire Regiment
Lt Colonel T.W.G. Stansfield

6th Battalion Green Howards
Lt Colonel G.C.P. Lance

7th Battalion the Green Howards
Lt Colonel A. Seagrim VC

151st Infantry Brigade

Brigadier J.E.S. Percy DSO MC

6th Battalion Durham Light Infantry
Lt Colonel W.I. Watson

8th Battalion Durham Light Infantry
Lt Colonel M.L.P. Jackson DSO

9th Battalion Durham Light Infantry.
Lt Colonel A. Clark DSO

1st Greek Brigade
Colonel Katsotos

2nd Free French Brigade
Lt Colonel Alessandrie

Royal Artillery.
Commander Brigadier H.R. Hall DSO MC

65th Field Regiment.
Lt Colonel J. St C. Holbrook

25th Light Anti-aircraft Regiment

Lt Colonel Orme

74th Field Regiment.
Lt Colonel Collett-White

111th Field Regiment
Lt Colonel J. Hill

124th Field Regiment
Colonel C.F. Todd

Royal Engineers.
Lt Colonel Lindsay

233rd Field Company
Major Osborne.

505th Field Company
Major J. Wood

Field Park Company
Major Revers

50th Division Signals.
Lt Colonel J. B de Lisle

2nd (Machine-gun) Battalion Cheshire Regiment.
Lt Colonel S.V. Keeling.

Bibliography

Battistelli P.P., *Battle Story: Alamein 1942* (Stroud: Spellmount, 2015)
Beckett, F.W., *Rommel; A Reappraisal* (Barnsley: Pen and Sword, 2013)
Brook, S., *Montgomery and the Eighth Army* (London: Bodley Head, 1991)

Clay, E.W., *The Path of the 50th: The Story of the 50th (Northumbrian) Division in the Second World War, 1939-1945* (Aldershot: Gale and Polden, 1950)

Davidson, E. and Manning D., *Chronology of World War Two* (London: Cassel, 1999)
Delaforce, P., *Monty's Northern Legions* (Stroud: Sutton, 2004)
Delaforce, P., *Churchill's Desert Rats* (Stroud: Sutton, 2002)

Evans, B., *Decisive Campaigns of the Desert Air Force* (Barnsley: Pen and Sword, 2014)

Ford, K., *El Alamein 1942* (Oxford: Osprey, 2005)

Garwood, L.M. *The Story of the 5th Battalion East Yorkshire Regiment* (Beverley: Highgate, 2002)
Graham A., *Sharpshooters at War* (London: Sharpshooters Regimental Association, 1964)

Hamilton, N., *Monty* (London: Hodder and Stoughton, 1981)
Harding, P., *From Gazala to Tunis* (Stroud: Fonthill, 2014)

Joslen, Lt Colonel H.F., *Orders of Battle 1939-1945* (London: HMSO, 1947)

Kershaw, R., *Tank Men* (London: Hodder and Stoughton, 2008)

Lee, D., *Up Close and Personal.* (Barnsley: Frontline Books, 2015)
Lewis, P. and English I.R., *Into Battle with the Durhams* (London: London Stamp Exchange, 1990)
Lucas, Philips C.E., *Alamein* (London: Heinemann, 1962)
Lucas, J., *War in the Desert* (London: Arms and Armour Press, 1982)
Lucas, J., *Panzer Army Africa*. (London, Purnell 1977)

Mitcham, S.W., *Rommel's Desert War* (Harrisburg, Pennsylvania: Stackpole Books, 2007)

Mitcham S.W., *Hitler's Legions* (London: Leo Cooper, 1985)

Mitchelhill-Green, D., *With Rommel in the Desert* (Barnsley: Pen and Sword, 2017)

Montgomery, B., *El Alamein to the River Sangro* (London: Hutchinson, 1948)

Montgomery, B., *Memoirs* (London: Companion Book Club, 1960)

Morisi, P., *The Italian Folgore Parachute Division in North Africa* (Solihull: Helion, 2016)

Moses H., *The Gateshead Gurkhas: 9th Durham Light Infantry* (Durham: County Durham Books 2001)

Moses, H., *The Faithful Sixth: 6th Durham Light Infantry* (Durham: County Durham Books 1995)

Nightingale, Lt Colonel P.R., *The East Yorkshire Regiment 1939 to 1945* (Howden: Mr Pye Books 1998)

Olive, M. and Edwards R., *Rommel's Desert Warriors* (Barnsley: Pen and Sword, 2012)

Playfair, Major General I.S.O., *The Mediterranean and the Middle East Vols. 3 & 4* (London: HMSO,1960)

Rissik, Major D., *The DLI at War* (Durham: Durham Light Infantry Depot, 1953)

Sadler, J., *El Alamein in the Soldier's Words* (London: Amberley, 2012)

Synge, Captain W.A.T., *The Story of the Green Howards 1939 to 1945* (Richmond: The Green Howards, 1952)

Thompson, J., D*esert Victory* (London: Ebury Press, 2012)

Urban, M., *The Tank War* (London: Abacus, 2013)

Warner, P., *Alamein* (Barnsley: Pen and Sword, 2007)

Willett, P., *Armoured Horseman* (Barnsley: Pen and Sword, 2014)

Index

Index of People

Index of Places

Index of Allied Units & Formations

Armies

Corps

Divisions

Brigades

Regiments

Other Forces and Formations

Index of Axis Units & Formations

Divisions

Other Forces & Formations

Index of War Materiel

Guns

Tanks

Aircraft

Other